D0344707

The 3 Big
Questions
for a
Frantic Family

Also by Patrick Lencioni

Leadership Fables

The Five Temptations of a CEO

The Four Obsessions of an Extraordinary Executive

The Five Dysfunctions of a Team

Death by Meeting

Silos, Politics, and Turf Wars

The Three Signs of a Miserable Job

Field Guide

Overcoming the Five Dysfunctions of a Team

The 3 Big Questions for a Frantic Family

A LEADERSHIP FABLE . . . ABOUT RESTORING SANITY TO THE MOST IMPORTANT ORGANIZATION IN YOUR LIFE

Patrick Lencioni

JOSSEY-BASS
A Wiley Imprint
www.josseybass.com

Published by Jossey-Bass
A Wiley Imprint
989 Market Street, San Francisco, CA 94103-1741—www.josseybass.com

Jossey-Bass books and products are available through most bookstores. To contact Jossey-Bass directly call our Customer Care Department within the U.S. at 800-956-7739, outside the U.S. at 317-572-3986, or fax 317-572-4002.

Jossey-Bass also publishes its books in a variety of electronic formats. Some content that appears in print may not be available in electronic books.

Library of Congress Cataloging-in-Publication Data

Lencioni, Patrick, 1965–
    The three big questions for a frantic family : a leadership fable—about restoring sanity to the most important organization in your life / Patrick Lencioni.
        p. cm.
    ISBN 978-0-7879-9532-4 (cloth)
    1. Family. 2. Family—Psychological aspects. I. Title.
    HQ519.L46 2008
    646.7'8—dc22

                                                                                    2008021041

Printed in the United States of America
FIRST EDITION
HB Printing   10 9 8 7 6 5 4 3 2 1

CONTENTS

For you, Laura, for who you are and what you do for all of us. And for mom and dad, for always putting family first.

INTRODUCTION

I need to start this book with two quick confessions.

First, I am not a family counselor or therapist, and I don't have a Ph.D. in psychology—or anything else for that matter. I'm a management consultant and business author, and more important, a husband and a father of four.

Second, I struggle with many books on family life. It's not that I don't enjoy the subject or find them interesting. It's just that they so often leave me feeling inadequate and overwhelmed by prescribing elaborate systems that can transform my family, as long as my wife and I have four days to invest up front and three hours per week to do follow-up exercises. Which, unfortunately, we don't.

So what prompted me to write this book?

Well, in my work as a consultant, I have frequently found myself in conversations with my clients about their families. I am happy to report that almost all the executives I've met claim that family is more important to them than work. And most of them seem to really mean it.

However, every one of those executives—including the one writing this book—would have to admit that they spend inordinately more time thinking about, strategizing about, and meeting about how to run their companies than they do their families. And yet they complain that life at home is far too reactive, frantic, and unfocused.

Of course, this makes no sense. Why would intelligent, family-oriented people overinvest in their work and fail to manage the most important organizations in their lives? And why wouldn't they apply any of the tools they use at work to improve the way their families function? I can think of a few reasons.

For one, it might not occur to us that management tools from the workplace can apply at home. We don't think about our families as organizations, and ourselves as the executives of those organizations. Additionally, I think many of us feel a little awkward, even embarrassed, at the thought of having a "strategic meeting" to talk about family values or strategic priorities. *Who does that, anyway?*

But more important than all of this, I think we under-manage our families because we take them for granted. Consider this:

Even the least organized among us spends time and energy planning and strategizing about our career, personal finances, and health. Why? Because we all think we might be forced to forfeit those things if we aren't purposeful and thoughtful about them. If we aren't proactive about managing our work and our career, we might wind up without a job. If we aren't strategic about our finances, we could watch our money disappear. And if we aren't purposeful about our exercise and diet, our health could fail us.

But when it comes to being purposeful, strategic, and proactive in our family life, we don't really see much risk of loss. Sure, we might have to deal with more stress and exhaustion than we'd like, but it's not going to threaten the existence of our families. And besides, every other family seems just as frantic as ours. Family chaos is just part of life, and so we accept levels of confusion and disorganization and craziness at home that we would not tolerate at work.

Sadly, it's not until people actually have to face the possibility of losing their families (through divorce or substance abuse or other serious behavioral problems) that they finally come to realize that a little planning and strategy would have been worthwhile. But by then they're spending hours and hours in painful discussions or counseling sessions just trying to recover what they're on the verge of losing. Which reinforces the importance of the old saying, "an ounce of prevention is worth a pound of cure."

Now don't get me wrong. I'm not suggesting that families can ever prevent or eliminate chaos and confusion completely from their lives. As long as there are sleepovers and in-laws and book reports and Little League games and proms and college applications and weddings to deal with, we will have unpredictability and craziness in our homes. And that's a good thing, because complete control—even if it were possible—would not be desirable. Life should be an adventure.

However, if we could achieve a little more sanity in the midst of that adventure, and transform our stressful, reactive, frantic families into more peaceful, proactive, and intentional ones, wouldn't that be worth doing? I certainly think so.

And that is the purpose of this little book—to help you run your family with more clarity and context and purposefulness by provoking you to answer three simple questions that can change your life. I hope you find my ideas helpful and that your family benefits from them in many ways for years to come.

The 3 Big Questions for a Frantic Family

The Fable

PART ONE

The
Problem

PROVOCATION

Theresa Cousins had never been so mad at her husband, Jude.

Ironically, the comment that sparked her anger wasn't really directed at her specifically and certainly wasn't meant as criticism. In fact, he said it without malice or emotion.

If my clients ran their companies the way we run this family, they'd be out of business.

That was it.

But as a full-time stay-at-home mom, Theresa couldn't help but feel like the target of the comment. Worse yet, she suspected that Jude might be right.

THERESA

The only sister among three brothers, Theresa Toscana considered herself a little tougher than most of her childhood friends. Receiving a partial scholarship to play volleyball at the University of Notre Dame, she chose mathematics as her major and made extra money by tutoring other athletes who were struggling with their freshman year calculus requirement.

One of those athletes was a tennis player who had a roommate named Jude Cousins, a fellow Californian who wasn't having much trouble with math but did need occasional advice about women. Even after she finished her tutoring assignment with his roommate, Theresa and Jude found excuses to be around each other. The two became friends, though they never dated.

After graduation, Theresa returned to her family's home in the San Francisco Bay Area, where she spent two and a half years in what she referred to as "accounting prison," bored to tears doing tax audits for companies that held no interest for her. So she went back to school to become a junior high school math teacher, something she would come to love.

It was during her first year in graduate school that she also reconnected with Jude.

REUNION

Having quickly abandoned his aspirations to be a journalist in Chicago, Jude joined the herds of recent college grads moving west to work in high tech. After finding a job with a growing software company, he quickly began climbing the corporate ladder, or more accurately, being pushed up it by an industry on fire.

Living with some college friends in San Francisco, Jude spent many Saturday mornings at a local Irish pub watching Notre Dame football games with fellow alumni. It was there that he saw Theresa, and after watching a disappointing loss, he agreed to have dinner with her at her parents' house that night.

Within a week, the old friends began dating, and five years later, to the relief of Theresa's mother, they were finally married.

For the next few years, Jude and Theresa worked hard at their jobs and enjoyed life in the City, eating out with friends and going to movies whenever they wanted. As much fun as that sounded, quietly they were struggling to start a family. Finally, after two and a half years of trying, Theresa became pregnant—with twins.

CONTINUOUS CHANGE

Almost to the day that they received the doubly overwhelming news from their doctor, Jude decided to leave his high-tech job and start his own consulting firm, working out of the spare bedroom in the couple's new little suburban home fifteen miles east of the City.

By the time the twins, Emily and Hailey, had their first birthday, Theresa had abandoned any plans for an imminent return to teaching, deciding that two infants would be more than enough work for a while.

And when she had Sophia a few years later, Theresa accepted that her teaching career would have to wait even longer, and that her role as a mother would be more than a full-time job. Besides, Jude's practice had grown much faster than they could have imagined, which meant he would be home to help less than she might have liked and that they would easily be able to afford their modest lifestyle on only one income.

When Sophia was ready to start preschool, Theresa thought life would slow down and allow her to breathe, and maybe even dive back into teaching part-time. Then along came Michael, born on Theresa's thirty-eighth birthday.

Just like that, Theresa Cousins found herself resuming a daily regimen that would fill her days and nights for the foreseeable future, with no achievable end in sight. It was more than she had expected, and would take its toll on her over the course of the next couple of years.

THE SCHEDULE

As the school year started and Theresa pondered the approach of her fortieth birthday less than four months away (on Christmas Eve), the Cousins family was in various states of full bloom. The twins were almost ten and were just beginning fourth grade, Sophia, nearly six, was entering kindergarten, and Michael, at one and a half, was still two years from preschool. The daily schedule at the Cousins household said it all.

Mondays were relatively easy, with swim practice and piano for the twins after school. Tuesdays were soccer practice for all the girls, which involved Jude coaching Hailey and Emily's squad, and Theresa helping out with Sophia's amoeba ball team. Wednesdays were the busiest days, with more swimming and a Girl Scout meeting for the twins, as well as Theresa's Bible study. Thursdays were Theresa's day to volunteer in the classroom, and another full soccer day, followed by a Friday that always seemed to involve a sleepover or a birthday party of some kind.

Saturdays were a logistics nightmare involving swim meets and soccer games and household chores, and an occasional recital, all with Michael in tow. Sundays were the calmest day of the week, reserved for church, and at least one soccer game or practice. And more often than not, Jude and Theresa had another family over for dinner or a barbecue, filling their house with no less than six kids, which was noisy but wonderful.

Add to that the daily homework, laundry, house cleaning, diapers, groceries, school board meetings, grandparents' visits, business trips, and the random illnesses or emotional crises that befall any houseful of four children, and the Cousins family was hanging on for dear life, with Theresa doing most of the hanging.

FEEBLE ATTEMPTS

ore and more frequently, Theresa and Jude found themselves engaged in a ritualistic conversation about the need
to find sanity in their schedule. Somehow the discussion
usually took place in the bathroom while Jude was shaving
or brushing his teeth, and would be prompted by Theresa
coming in to remind her husband about an unexpected or
forgotten item on the schedule that day.

"Don't forget about the parent-teacher meeting tonight,"
or "The twins' scrimmage in Walnut Creek starts at six-thirty."

Jude would stop what he was doing, take a deep
breath, and announce, "We *have* to cut back our activities."

"I would love to," Theresa would respond sincerely
though somewhat hopelessly. "What can we stop doing?"

And then the husband and wife would proceed to review the various activities on their calendar, justifying each
one as being important enough to keep doing, or lament-
ing a commitment that they had already made from which
they couldn't escape.

"Classroom volunteering keeps me involved at school, which I think is important," Theresa would explain.

Jude would nod his head and ask, "Can't we take the twins out of piano? What were we thinking when we signed them up for that?"

"Well, we've always said that the girls need some sort of music, and they really like it. At least Hailey does, and she won't do it if Emily doesn't."

Jude would gently correct her. "Actually, I think it was *you* who always said that they need music lessons."

She would pause, and change the subject. "Maybe we should stop swimming."

Jude would consider it, for a moment. "But isn't every one of the girls' friends in swimming? That's half their social life right there. And ours, for that matter."

Theresa would agree and then add, "And I definitely don't want to stop doing Bible study."

"Absolutely not," Jude would affirm. "In fact, I should start going too. I need to figure out how to free up my time on Wednesday mornings."

Theresa would sigh, "I don't know what else we can change. Sometimes I just want to move to the country and live like the Waltons."

Jude would bow his head in a defeated sign of agreement, and then come to life as though he had a sudden brainstorm.

"Here's an idea." He'd pause, for effect. "Let's stop changing Michael's diapers! That will save us at least an hour a day. Sure, it will be messy, but I think it'll be worth it."

Theresa would laugh, and then Jude would look at the little clock in the bathroom. "Ooh, I'm going to be late."

He'd kiss his wife and hustle out the door with a "See you at soccer!" or "I'll pick up Sophia from swimming!" or "Remember, I'm out of town tomorrow night so I can't go to the recital!"

And yet another day of chaos would begin.

Some days Theresa would find herself longing for what her father-in-law annoyingly called a "real job." But she knew that this would be her full-time vocation for much of the next decade, and she had decided long ago to take it more seriously than any paid position she'd ever had.

Which is probably why the comment her husband was about to make set her hair on fire.

SENSITIVITY

They had just put the last of the kids to bed and were cleaning the kitchen. Theresa mentioned a missed dentist appointment and the fee they'd have to pay as a result. And that prompted Jude's infamous remark.

"If my clients ran their companies the way we run this family, they'd go out of business."

Knowing his wife's passionate nature and her family's Italian heritage, Jude wouldn't normally have been surprised by a slightly fiery response to an offhanded comment. But the magnitude of Theresa's reaction, especially given the absence of any malice on his part, caught him off guard.

After only a brief moment of icy silence, Theresa pounced. "And what is that supposed to mean?"

"Nothing. It's just that—"

She interrupted. "So you think you could do a better job at this, I guess?"

Jude was stunned by the unusually harsh tone in his wife's voice. "I didn't say that."

"But you'd fire me if I were the CEO of one of your companies?"

Jude smiled, a little nervously, and made a weak attempt at a joke. "Well, first of all, they're not *my* companies. They're my clients, so I can't fire anyone even if—"

"You know what I mean," she interrupted.

Jude remained calm. "Second, I wasn't saying that you're doing a bad job. I'm just saying that everything is always so—"

He hesitated, searching for the right word. "Crazy."

"And you think that's my fault?"

Jude shook his head, took a deep breath, and did his best to calm the situation. "Now, wait a second, Theresa."

It didn't work.

"No, you wait a second. I bust my butt day after day after day, and you have the gall to compare me to one of your clients?" She didn't wait for a response. "Let me tell you something, Jude. I don't have an administrative assistant or a private jet or an expense account or a limo driver. It's just me and four kids and a husband, all of whom think that everything just gets taken care of magically. Well it doesn't. It's hard work and it never stops."

Jude hesitated, not wanting to further exacerbate the situation. Desperate for relief, he tried humor again. In a playfully sarcastic tone, he corrected his wife. "By the way, none of my clients have private jets."

At first Theresa looked like she was going to blow again. Until Jude smiled sheepishly and forced her to do the same. For just a moment.

Calming down now, but still upset, Theresa explained. "You know what I mean, Jude. I have never worked harder at anything in my life, and it's not working. You don't think that's hard to hear?"

Now she was on the verge of tears, so Jude chose his words carefully.

"What do you mean, it's not working? I didn't mean to put this all on you. I didn't say 'if my clients ran their companies the way *you* ran this family'; I said *we*."

Theresa shook her head. "Come on. I know we're partners here, but most of the stuff you're talking about, the chaos, the stress, has to do with my part of the job. Your part of it is all tidy and neat. You make enough money for us, you come to the big events, you tuck the girls in at night. You're their knight in shining armor . . . and I'm the warden of the jail."

"That's not fair, Theresa. You're more than a warden." He paused. "You're also the cook, the janitor, the bus driver, the—"

Now Theresa hit her husband playfully in the arm, but with some force.

After more than a decade of marriage, Jude knew when to offer an apology, even if he hadn't meant to do anything wrong. "I'm sorry, Theresa. I should have thought about what I was saying."

He hesitated for a moment, unsure about whether he should say what he was thinking. "I know life is crazy for you. And I have to tell you, it is for me too. I come home every night, and between work and soccer and homework and everything else my head never seems to stop spinning." He hesitated again before asking the next question. "But is it really that bad for you?"

Theresa sighed. "It's not that it's bad. It's just overwhelming. And I don't want to complain, because I realize how blessed I am. It's just hard right now. I'll be fine."

Jude wasn't quite convinced. "Are you unhappy, though?"

Theresa shook her head and took a breath. "How can I be unhappy? I actually enjoy most of what I'm doing. I'm just frustrated."

Now Jude was relieved, but a little confused.

Theresa continued without pausing. "I mean, I love picking the girls up from school and talking to them in the minivan on the way home and making Michael laugh when I change his diaper and coaching Sophia in soccer and I wouldn't even mind the laundry and cleaning if I had time to do it the way I'd like to, but throw it all together and mix in the distractions and the tattling and the surprise visits from relatives and the school politics and everything else and it gets so hurried and overwhelming that I can't pause long enough to enjoy the moment."

She finally stopped for a breath, exhausted and emotional just thinking about her life. "And that is the real shame. I'm not enjoying doing things I've always wanted to do."

Jude put his arms around his wife and didn't say anything for a long ten seconds. Finally he offered, "You know, I bet every other family we know is in the same situation. It's just part of having a handful of active kids and living in this kind of environment."

Though her anger at Jude had all but dissipated, Theresa wasn't ready to let herself off the hook.

She pulled back a little so she could look her husband in the eye. "I don't think everyone has this problem, Jude. Do you think that the Marshes do? Or the Horans? There is no way that Kelly Horan feels like I do."

Jude smiled. "I bet you'd be surprised."

At that moment Theresa decided she was going to find out for herself.

RESEARCH

Theresa couldn't believe she was doing it. For the first time ever, she felt like her crazy Aunt Stella. Theresa was calling Kelly Horan to find out if her life was as out of control as her own.

Though they were acquaintances of the Cousins family, the Horans were certainly not close friends. Theresa had used Kelly as an example in her discussion with Jude because she had a reputation for being one of those perfect moms. That reputation made her the object of good-natured envy and humor among some of the mothers at school, all of whom knew Kelly to be consistently gracious, if not a little shy. The Horans had an immaculate house and yard. Kelly's hair and clothes were never out of style or unkempt. Worse yet, her three kids, from the toddler to the teenager, always seemed to be well-behaved at school and at church.

Theresa would normally have felt more than a little awkward about asking another mom her secrets—especially one she didn't know well—because she wouldn't want to come across as nosy or desperate. But she was, in fact, desperate for help.

The call would be shorter than she could have imagined.

KIMONO OPENING

As soon as Theresa explained why she was calling, Kelly cut her off in her barely perceptible Mississippi accent.

"Theresa, I would be glad to help you. But I'm afraid that you're going to have to come over if I'm going to be of any real use to you."

As strange as that sounded, Theresa wasn't in any position to turn down the offer, not after putting herself out there as she had. And so, eleven minutes later, she was parking her minivan in front of the Horan house, which, of course, was immaculate.

Kelly greeted Theresa more warmly than she had ever done at school or church, and seemed genuinely glad to have her in her home. It was as neat and clean as it was stylishly decorated.

How can this be? Theresa wondered as she surveyed the tidy kitchen and family room. *She has three boys!*

"So, you want to talk to me about how I run my home life?" Kelly seemed confused. "Is that right?"

Theresa nodded, a little embarrassed now. "Well, yes. I mean, I'm just wondering if there's anything you do that helps you, I don't know—"

Before she could finish, Kelly interrupted sweetly. "Why in heaven's name did you decide to call me?"

Theresa paused to choose her words carefully. "Well, you are one of the calmest, most put-together people I know."

Kelly digested the comment dispassionately. "Who else have you talked to about this?"

"About coming here?"

Kelly smiled. "No, who else have you asked advice from?"

Theresa shook her head. "No one."

Now Kelly seemed genuinely shocked. "So you're telling me that I am the first person you decided to talk to about how to improve the way you run your home and family?" She sounded delightedly incredulous.

Theresa nodded, prompting Kelly Horan to grab her by the hand. "Come with me, friend."

Before she knew what was happening, Kelly was leading Theresa up a staircase and into a hallway with four closed doors.

Bringing her toward the door at the end of the narrow room, Kelly took a breath and smiled. "If you tell anyone about this, I will have to kill you."

And with that she flung open her bedroom door.

After Theresa overcame a mild sense of shock, she took in the entire scene.

The bed was unmade, a tornado of sheets and pillows. Small stacks of paper and what appeared to be envelopes surrounded a wicker trashcan in the middle of the room. At least four piles of dirty or perhaps clean and wrinkled laundry covered the ground at the foot of the bed. Folded stacks of shirts, underwear, and socks covered a desk on the far wall.

The place was the definition of a mess.

Looking toward the bathroom, Theresa saw an unidentifiable structure that was covered with towels and sheets.

"That's my treadmill," Kelly explained. "I use it to dry towels when the dryer breaks. And you don't even want to go into the bathroom."

Theresa could not believe the words that came out of her mouth next. "Oh, yes I do."

Kelly laughed out loud. "Okay. But enter at your own risk."

Theresa made her way through the maze of clothes and debris in the bedroom, and arrived at the entrance to the bathroom. What she saw was impressive.

The counter next to the sink was covered with open mascara bottles and cotton swabs. At least half the drawers were open, revealing a random collection of toothpaste tubes, hair brushes, and a can of shaving cream. Magazines were scattered around the toilet.

Theresa turned and saw Kelly standing in the doorway, smiling ear to ear. "Like what I've done with the place?" They laughed.

Next, she brought her guest downstairs again, and opened a door near the kitchen. Again, Theresa had to look for a few seconds to believe what she was seeing.

It was the garage, but there were no cars inside. Instead, the room was filled, wall to wall and halfway up to the ceiling, with boxes and crates and Christmas lights and paint cans and sporting goods.

"If you look closely," Kelly explained, "you can see a hidden path that allows you to make your way to the other side. But you have to be very flexible and athletic to get there."

Finally, Kelly brought Theresa back to the kitchen where they sat down to talk. "So now you know how I keep the rest of the house clean."

Theresa suddenly felt the need to match her host's openness and counterbalance her admissions of guilt.

"Okay, so you've got a few messy rooms. I've got messy rooms of my own, but I've also got a filthy car, two years of Christmas cards that have never been sent, a blinking light on my minivan that says I'm two hundred miles late on my next oil change, a case of sleep deprivation that will take five years to unpack, two daughters who are suddenly fascinated with boys, another who won't eat anything but Cheerios and tangerines, and a son who's approaching two and shows no interest in talking. On top of that, one of my sisters is mad at me but won't tell me why, I'm fifteen pounds overweight, I can't decide if I'm being too tough or too lenient with my kids, and my husband thinks I'm lazy."

Kelly tried not to laugh but couldn't help it. "He didn't really say you were lazy, did he?"

Theresa shook her head. "No. But sometimes I think he thinks it. Or maybe I just think it. I don't know."

Kelly smiled, but this time a little sadly. "Theresa Cousins, the things you don't know."

Theresa didn't dare ask, but Kelly had already decided to tell her about the challenges in the Horan family. Their oldest son, a freshman, had been suspended from the high school swim team for drinking a beer at a party. The middle son was flunking third-grade math, and Tim, Kelly's husband, needed to have his hip replaced at age forty-five. On top of that, they were waiting to find out if their identity had been stolen by someone with a penchant for buying jewelry on the home shopping network.

"Honey, no one has a perfect life."

"I know, Kelly. And I don't want mine to be perfect. I just want it to be more manageable."

"Well, when you figure out how to make that happen, please make me your first phone call again."

Theresa smiled and agreed, not realizing how soon she'd be calling.

DATA POINTS

Strangely buoyed by her visit with Kelly Horan, Theresa continued her research in spite of the mounting laundry and dishes and other daily responsibilities at home. Her next subject: Alison Marsh.

Taking a slight detour on her way home from Kelly's, Theresa drove past the Marsh house and was pleasantly surprised to see Alison getting out of her Suburban with an armful of groceries.

Alison's kids were older than Theresa's, and five years earlier she had decided to go back to work part-time as a speech teacher at a local community college. The combination of her work life and all the activities in her family made it something of a rarity to catch her at home. As it turned out, this happened to be one of Alison's rare days off, and she was using it to catch up on household chores and maintenance.

Theresa had a closer relationship with Alison than she did with Kelly, so she didn't hesitate to pull over and say hello. Before she knew what was happening, she was in the house helping Alison put away groceries and telling her about the research she was doing.

As it turned out, the Marsh family was almost nothing like the Horans. And in some ways, very similar.

From a physical standpoint, Alison's home was anything but perfect. A baseball glove and a bat on the front lawn. A little clutter here and there in the family room. Shoes and cleats discarded on the floor near the door going to the garage.

When asked about her approach to running the house and the family, Alison's answer was typical of most parents, as Theresa would come to learn.

"Approach? I don't know. We just do what needs to be done until everyone's in bed and we can rest. Then we get up the next day to do it again." She laughed, in a resigned kind of way.

The three Marsh kids were involved in as many activities as the Cousins', if not more, which meant that Alison spent just about half her time in that Suburban. She complained about her husband signing the boys up for too many sports out of fear that they'd fall behind their friends, and leaving it to her to get them from one practice to another.

Scott Marsh was an orthopedist in San Francisco, which meant he kept regular office hours. Unlike Jude, whose consulting firm was located just a few miles from home and whose schedule varied greatly day to day, he was rarely available to help with any daytime responsibilities.

Alison vented. "Scott's home less and less these days, and he can't stand the managing doc—who's driving the practice into the ground. On top of all that, his commute is a nightmare."

"At least he doesn't travel," Theresa said wistfully. "When Jude's out of town, it throws everything off. And when he comes home, it gets worse before it gets better."

Alison agreed. "Yeah, we've all got our challenges. Except, I suppose, if you're like Suzie Martin or Kelly Horan."

Theresa smiled. "I think we'd be surprised."

"Yeah. Now that you mention it, Suzie did say that they had a rough patch in their marriage last year, which shocked me because they always seem like the perfect couple with the perfect kids."

"You know, sometimes I think it would be better if people stopped dressing up to go out and being on their best behavior in public. Then we'd all stop thinking everyone else was perfect."

Alison considered it for a second. "And I wish they'd stop cleaning their house when someone is coming over to visit. Scott always comments on how clean people's houses are, and I tell him that our house is always clean when people come over, too."

"That's the same conversation that Jude and I have, almost word for word."

They laughed.

Theresa suddenly frowned in thought. "One more question, and then I'll leave you alone."

Alison waved her hand as if to say *you're not bothering me.*

"Do you think this is just a function of having so many kids? I mean, do you think families with one or two manage to avoid all this stress?"

Alison gave it some thought as she put cans in her cupboard. "I don't know. My sister has two little girls. She and her husband are as crazy as we are, and always complaining about how tired they are. I don't think it really matters that much."

"That makes sense," Theresa added. "It's not like things were any less hectic before Sophia was born."

Alison laughed. "Yeah, we used to think we were tired before we had kids."

Theresa laughed too, thanked her friend for her time, and headed home. As she drove she felt a bizarre mix of relief and hopelessness, a feeling that would last only until Sunday.

BARBECUE

As usual, it wasn't until Saturday that Jude remembered to tell his wife that he had invited people over for a barbecue the next afternoon. Fortunately for him, Theresa was actually excited about the invitees, and so she let him off the hook with a gentle reprimand.

Rob Groninger was one of Jude's most senior consultants at the firm, and one of his first hires. His personality was a rare combination of analytical skepticism and irrepressible optimism, something that suited him well for consulting. Rob and his wife, Linda, had two daughters of similar age to the Cousins twins, and though they lived in another town more than a half hour away, the families had become close friends and were always welcome guests.

Not long after the Groningers arrived, Theresa found herself in the kitchen with Rob putting chicken and vegetables on kabob spears. He knew her well enough to tease his boss's wife. "So I hear that Jude stuck his foot right down his throat the other day."

"He told you?"

Rob laughed. "If we're talking about the 'if my clients ran their companies the way—'"

She interrupted. "Yep, that's the one." She laughed too. "What exactly did he say?"

"Not much. Just that he didn't realize that it would make you so—" he hesitated, and she finished the sentence for him.

"Pissed off?"

He laughed again. "In fact, I think that's exactly what he said."

"Yeah, I think I overreacted a little. But it was not the smartest comment in the world."

At that moment Linda Groninger came into the kitchen. "What wasn't the smartest comment?" She too knew Theresa well enough to be a little nosy.

Theresa tried to explain. "Oh, just something that Jude said to me a few days ago about—"

"You mean the 'if my clients ran their companies the way you run this house' comment?"

Theresa was a little surprised, looking at Rob. "So I guess you told her, too."

He smiled. "Oh yeah, I told her. And we almost got into the same argument that you guys did."

Theresa was animated now. "Oh, I've got to hear this."

Rob and Linda did their best to recount the conversation, at times almost slipping back into the actual argument.

Eventually, the topic of the discussion shifted to the overwhelming nature of raising children.

Linda tried to explain the mystery of her stress. "I've always wondered why I'm so overwhelmed with just two girls to worry about, and why my parents seemed to do fine with five kids. And then I read an article last week that said raising two kids today is like raising four or five thirty years ago. Between the play dates and the formal activities and the academic pressure and the Internet, parenting is a lot harder than when my mom sent us out into the neighborhood and said 'be home by dinner.'"

Theresa was glad to know that her struggle was not just about adding little Michael to the mix. She was also relieved to know that working moms like Linda had many of the same challenges as stay-at-home moms like herself.

Unfortunately, before they could get any further into the interesting conversation, Jude came in from the patio to remind them that dinner had to be cooked and the kids had to be fed. But the topic would not disappear for long.

THE RESURFACING

When dinner was over and the girls were in the den watching a movie and little Michael was asleep, the adults went to the living room to play cards. Linda didn't hesitate to pick up the conversation from the kitchen, taking a jab at Jude.

"So, Jude. Exactly what is it that your clients do that we don't?"

Jude was caught completely off guard. "What do you mean?"

Rob laughed. "We were talking about your big foot-in-mouth comment."

Jude smiled. "Oh, you were, huh?"

Linda teased him. "I can't believe you were so harsh."

Jude defended himself by clarifying that he wasn't trying to put the blame on Theresa. "I said, 'the way *we* run this family.'"

"But you had to know that's how she would take it," Linda pushed back playfully.

Jude shook his head. "No, I guess I'm really that clueless. I honestly didn't mean it that way, but I apologized, and I won't do it again. Let's play cards."

Linda started shuffling, but Theresa wasn't ready to let go yet. She turned to Jude.

"But what is it that your clients do?"

Jude was just a little defensive now. "Come on, Theresa. I said I was sorry."

Theresa reached out and touched her husband's knee. "I'm not asking because I'm mad, Jude. I really want to know."

Accepting the sincerity of her intentions, Jude entertained the question. "But you already know what our clients do. You've been around since I started the firm."

"Well, I guess I have an idea. But since Sophia was born, we actually don't talk about it that much. And for all I know, you're doing something completely new."

"It hasn't changed that much," Jude explained.

Rob saved the day. "I tell you what. Come by the office sometime this week, and I'll take you through our approach in a half hour."

"What a gentleman you are, Rob." Theresa looked at her husband as if to say, *why didn't you offer to do that?*

Rob confessed. "Actually, I'm just sick of talking about it, and I want to play cards."

Theresa relented and let the game begin, not realizing that she would be taking Rob up on his offer before lunch the next day.

CHAOS

I started at breakfast—when Sophia proceeded to throw up her Honey Nut Cheerios onto her little brother. After she and Jude cleaned the mess, Theresa called the doctor to make arrangements to take her in later that morning. While she was on hold, Jude returned to the kitchen pulling a rolling suitcase behind him.

"What's that for?"

"I'm going to Vancouver."

"I didn't know that."

"I sent you an e-mail last week, and it's on the calendar."

"Which calendar?"

"The one in the bedroom."

Now she was annoyed. "That's not the family calendar. The one over there is." She pointed to the small desk in the kitchen.

"But I thought that's where you keep the vacation schedule."

"Yeah, the long-term stuff we put on the bedroom calendar. The day-to-day stuff goes out here. You know that."

Jude sighed.

"When do you get back?" Theresa pressed him.

"Tomorrow. Late."

"What about the school board meeting?"

"What about it? I'm not on the school board. You are."

"Yeah, but I told them you'd talk to them about strategic planning."

Suddenly Jude remembered. "Oh, right. I remember you saying something about that. I thought you called my office and had them put it on my schedule."

"I thought I did too. Sometimes I'm not sure they follow through on that stuff. This is the third time this has happened."

Jude took a deep breath. "Let me see if there is any way I can move my flight up and get back in time for the meeting. It's not going to be easy, though."

"Well, either way I need a babysitter. Can you ask Bill if one of his girls can do it?"

Jude was getting a little frustrated now. "I don't even know if Bill's in town and whether I can get ahold of him. And I've got a pretty full plate today. Why don't you call Nora?"

Theresa responded sarcastically, as she cleaned up vomit from the table while holding her one-year-old. "You're right, my plate's not that full."

"That's not what I meant. It's just that I'm—"

He looked at the clock.

"I'm going to miss my flight if I don't get out of here. Listen, I'm sorry. This is a crazy day. We can talk about it tonight when I get to my hotel. Hang in there. I hope Sophia feels better."

He kissed Theresa and moved toward the door.

"Have a good flight. Try to call before the girls go to bed so we can say prayers on the phone."

"Will do."

And he was gone.

Theresa looked at the clock, and then at her kitchen, and under her breath said, "Lord, please help me get through this day."

APPOINTMENTS

Theresa's beloved pediatrician, Dr. Robbins, agreed to see Sophia that morning, and so by ten o'clock they were sitting in the waiting room. Thankfully, Sophia was already looking better, flipping through some of the kids' magazines in the play area.

Theresa decided to grab a few minutes of reading herself, and after sorting through a stack of *Parents* and *People* and *Pediatrics Today* and a host of other magazines that all seemed to begin with the letter *P*, she settled on one called *Plain and Simple*. She had seen it in the grocery store and had always been drawn to its neat, tidy, and orderly look and feel. Today was a day when orderliness was particularly attractive.

After flipping through the various ads and articles, Theresa came upon something that caught her eye. Titled "The Art of Balance," it was a story about a Hollywood actress who, one year earlier, had given birth to twins. The point of the feature was that this busy actress was managing to balance her life of celebrity with her role as a mother.

The lead picture showed the ridiculously thin actress standing on a low balance beam, tranquilly smiling with her eyes closed, holding her babies in each arm, extended as though she were using them to keep herself steady.

The caption was a quote from the actress: "Soy and Raisin have given me a sense of peace that I never had when I was living for myself. They force me to be more disciplined, more focused."

After she had stopped trying to figure out whether Raisin was the girl or the boy, Theresa forced herself to read the story. Though she was not accustomed to keeping up with the lives of the rich and famous, her curiosity was piqued because of the twins angle, and because she was desperate for some kind of balance in her own life. *Maybe I'll learn something,* she thought to herself.

The article began by reviewing the film credits of the actress, and those of her husband, a director. Amazingly, during the year following the birth of the twins, the actress had filmed a movie and had already begun work on a second, while the father of the twins had been in Africa for three months making a movie himself. Coincidentally, he was directing his wife's new film.

The writer of the article then described how the new parents had decided that raising their children and providing them with a loving home were their top priorities, but that they didn't feel they had to sacrifice their careers in order to do that. The article went on to explain the secrets to their success, which is what set Theresa's hair on fire.

The actress was employing two and a half FTEs. Luckily for Theresa, the writer provided an explanation for the acronym: Full-Time Equivalents. Essentially, Soy and Raisin had two nannies on staff at all times, and one that came in every other day for more focused 'teaching.' Beyond that, the starlet had a cook, a personal trainer, a driver, and a daily housekeeper to tidy things up when the family was in town.

Fortunately, before Theresa's head exploded with frustration, a nurse came into the waiting room and announced that Dr. Robbins was ready to see Sophia.

DIAGNOSIS

After a quick examination, he determined that Theresa's littlest girl was not really sick, but that her vomiting might be a function of some kind of food reaction. And when he found out that she also struggled with asthma, he recommended that she see an allergy specialist.

"How can she have a food allergy? She only eats Cheerios and tangerines."

He smiled. "Just take her to Dr. Jacobs. He'll take you through a battery of tests to determine what's going on."

Theresa knew Dr. Robbins well enough to vent a little. "Oh, terrific, another appointment."

He smiled.

"And if she is allergic to something, then what?"

"Well, it's probably nothing. But if it is a food allergy, she'll have to avoid eating whatever's causing it, of course. If she has a grass or pollen-related allergy, then you might be able to do a series of shots to reduce it."

Theresa sighed. "Is that where she'd have to go to the doctor twice a week for a few months, and then once a week for a year, and then—" She didn't finish the sentence.

"I'm afraid so. But after a couple of years, she'll just need it once a month. But we're getting ahead of ourselves. Go see Dr. Jacobs."

Theresa thanked Dr. Robbins and apologized for her mood.

"Oh, I hear it all the time. Don't worry. You've got the most stressful job in the world, and I think you're entitled to complain from time to time."

Theresa appreciated his understanding, but wasn't as comforted by it as she would have liked to have been. As she climbed into her minivan for the drive home, she muttered to herself, *I don't want the most stressful job in the world.*

"What did you say, mommy?" Sophia asked.

"Nothing, honey. Just talking to myself."

DETOUR

he doctor's office was less than a mile from Jude's office, and Theresa would have to drive within a few blocks of it to get back to the freeway. So she decided to stop by and say hello to her husband, forgetting that he was out of town.

As she and Sophia came through the front door and approached the reception desk, Theresa saw Rob sitting in a conference room alone, apparently having a conversation with someone on a speakerphone. As soon as he saw her, he waved.

Nancy at reception greeted her guests with extra enthusiasm. "Well hello there, Sophia. Did you come in to have lunch with me?" Nancy had joined Cousins Consulting a few weeks before Sophia was born, and thus had developed a particular fondness for her boss's red-headed five-year-old.

"No. We went to the doctor because I threw up on my brother."

Nancy laughed. "Well I hope you're okay."

Theresa answered for her daughter. "She's fine. But the doctor said she might have a food allergy of some kind."

And then it dawned on Theresa that her husband was out of town. "Oh, I forgot that Jude's in Vancouver today."

Nancy pretended to be dejected. "Oh, and I thought you came in to see me."

At that moment Rob exited the conference room and scooped up Sophia in his arms. "No way. She came to see me."

Sophia giggled. "No, silly. I came to see my daddy."

Theresa joined the conversation. "I forgot about his trip."

With Sophia still in his arms he responded, "I thought you might be taking me up on my lecture offer from last night."

It took Theresa a moment to remember what he was talking about.

Rob encouraged her. "I could do it right now, over lunch. We can bring in sandwiches, right, Nancy?"

"Sure, and Sophia can sit up here with me and color and help answer the phones."

Sophia was sold. "Yes, yes, yes. Please, mommy."

Theresa hesitated at first. "Well, I've got the sitter until one o'clock and, at this point, it doesn't make sense for me to bring Sophia to school. Why not?"

Nancy took Theresa's and Sophia's orders for sandwiches, and as soon as Sophia was settled in with her crayons at the reception desk, Theresa made her way to the conference room for what would turn out to be one of the most important lectures of her life.

PART TWO

Business School

OVERVIEW

ob stood at the whiteboard like a professor, more enthusiastic about his assignment than Theresa would have guessed.

"Okay, Theresa. You're smart, and you have a pretty good understanding of what Jude and I do, so I'm going to move pretty fast and let you stop me if you have any questions. But you have to promise that you'll ask if something doesn't make sense. All right?"

Theresa nodded. "Just remember, my mind has been stuck in diapers and carpools and preschool for the past nine years. Don't assume I know too much."

"I think you'll do fine. As Jude always says, what we do is extraordinarily simple."

Theresa nodded to indicate she'd heard her husband say that many times.

Rob began. "One of the most important things we do, maybe the most important, is helping companies achieve what we call *organizational clarity.*"

He wrote the two words on the whiteboard. "If the executives who lead an organization are not clear and on the same page about how to answer a number of basic questions, they cannot possibly be successful."

"What kinds of questions?" Theresa wanted to know.

Before Rob could answer, Nancy came into the conference room.

Theresa was suddenly concerned. "How is Sophia doing? Is she keeping you away from your work?"

Nancy smiled. "Not at all. She's a joy. I just wanted to let you know that Jude's on the phone."

"Who does he want to talk to?" asked Theresa.

"Both of you. He's on line three."

Nancy left and Rob pushed a button and activated the speakerphone. He let Theresa talk first.

"Hey there, honey. How was your flight?"

"It was fine. A few minutes late, actually. I'm on my way to the hotel right now."

Rob chimed in, teasing. "Hi, honey. How's the weather in Vancouver?"

"It's raining, sweetie."

Theresa shook her head at the goofy men.

Jude changed the subject. "Hey, if you guys are going to be getting together behind my back, at least pick someplace a little more discreet."

They laughed.

"What are you doing at the office today, Theresa?"

She explained about the doctor appointment and how she forgot that Jude was out of town, and how Rob and Nancy had talked her into staying for lunch and the lecture.

"I bet you're taking copious notes," Jude teased his wife.

Rob explained, "We just got started but she's got her pad and paper ready to go."

Theresa teased back. "Ask Jude who got better grades in college. And then ask him who takes better notes."

They laughed, until Jude said that he had an appointment in twenty minutes and had to go.

After saying their good-byes, Rob and his pupil resumed the lesson.

"Okay, where were we?"

Good student that she was, Theresa reminded him. "We were talking about the questions that an executive team has to answer in order to achieve organizational clarity."

"Right. So, there are six questions." He went to the board and began to write them down as Theresa transcribed them all.

1. What is the ultimate reason you're in business? (core purpose)

2. What are the essential characteristics that are inherent in your organization and that you could never knowingly violate? (core values)

3. What specifically does your company do, and for whom? (business definition)

4. How do you go about doing what you do in a way that differentiates you from your competitors and gives you an advantage? (strategy)

5. What is your biggest priority, and what do you need to accomplish to achieve it? (goals)

6. Who has to do what to achieve your goals? (roles and responsibilities)

CORE PURPOSE

As soon as they were done writing, they dove in, spending the better part of the next hour going over some of the nuances related to the six questions on the board, and reviewing as many examples from clients and other high-profile companies as they could.

"The core purpose at Mary Kay Cosmetics has nothing to do with makeup—it's all about giving women opportunities in business," Rob explained. "And Nike's core purpose is about giving customers a sense of being a competitor. Southwest Airlines, on the other hand, has a more direct core purpose: to make travel affordable for everyone."

"Why does an organization really need a core purpose?" Theresa asked.

"Well, companies need to remember why they exist so they don't lose their way and start getting into markets and businesses that aren't consistent with what they're all about. And they need to give their employees a sense of purpose. If you don't care about women having business opportunities, you shouldn't work at Mary Kay and they shouldn't hire you. And if you're not a big believer in competitive sports, Nike isn't going to be someplace where you're excited about going to work."

Theresa nodded her head, though she could have asked a few more questions. "I don't think I need to worry about this for our family. The purpose is pretty clear. And I don't have much time, so I think we ought to move on to the next one."

Rob was glad to oblige.

CORE VALUES

"The key to core values is not having too many of them. Companies tend to get this wrong by compiling a list of five or ten or fifteen words that all sound nice but aren't really an accurate, fundamental part of the real culture."

"Why do they do that?" Theresa seemed particularly curious about this topic.

"Because they want to cover all their bases, and they confuse core values with other kinds."

"I think I remember Jude talking about this a few years ago. What are the other kinds of values?"

"Aspirational, permission-to-play, and accidental."

"This sounds a little complicated."

"It's not. Just start by focusing on core values. Those are the traits or qualities that are fundamental parts of an organization's culture. You don't make them up, you just look around and describe what's already true. Forget what you wish you were, or what the perfect family next door is, and focus on what you are at your core."

Theresa smiled and continued writing. "Keep going," she said.

"Aspirational values, on the other hand, are the ones you wish you had because it would make your organization better."

"But it's not necessarily a reality, right?"

"In fact, it's not a reality by definition, which is why an organization would aspire to adopt it."

"What about the next one? Permission to—?"

"Permission-to-play. Those are the values that often seem generic, because in reality they're the minimum standards for working at a company. Without them, you don't have permission to play, or work, at a company. Honesty. Respect. Integrity. That kind of thing. Very few companies can honestly say that honesty and respect are their core values, but that's a longer story for another time."

Theresa nodded and wrote down what he was saying, so Rob continued with the last kind of values that get confused with the core.

"Accidental values are those that aren't necessarily good for a company, but exist. Sometimes they have to be eliminated or closely watched."

"For instance?"

"Like here at our firm. There was a time when everyone we hired had little kids. We'd talk about poopy diapers and Little League and kindergarten all the time. After a while we wondered whether a nonparent would be comfortable here, like a recent college grad or a semi-retired person or someone who was single. We felt like we might be missing out on people who shared our core values but didn't necessarily share our accidental value of parenthood."

"So it's not necessarily a bad thing."

"Not at all. Being a parent is awesome. It's just not a requirement for fitting into our firm."

"Unless it's part of your core."

"Exactly." Rob went back to the lesson. "So, when you confuse your core values with your aspirational, permission-to-play, and accidental ones, you end up with a very long list of generic-sounding values that only inspire cynicism among employees—who think the executives are in denial about the real culture of the company."

Now Theresa got it. "Yeah, a few weeks ago I saw a sign in the elevator of a hospital that said their core values were . . . ," she thought about it for a moment before slowly ticking off the ones she could remember, "innovation, quality, teamwork, customer service, patient care, integrity, financial responsibility." She hesitated, before continuing, "They also had community service and diversity and environmentalism in there."

They laughed.

Rob continued. "And that's what makes people cynical about values."

Theresa seemed to be arriving at something. "You know, for all the talk you hear about family values, no one ever really says what they are. I've got to believe that figuring out what a family's core values are would make things a lot clearer."

Rob nodded. "I haven't really thought about it like that before, but I think that makes a lot of sense."

Theresa was excited now. "Okay, I'm feeling good about values. Let's move on."

BUSINESS DEFINITION

"The next thing is the business definition. That's just a simple, one-sentence description of what a company actually does. Without adverbs or fancy words."

"Can you give me some examples?"

"Sure. Nike designs, manufactures, markets, and sells shoes, athletic apparel, and equipment. Southwest Airlines flies passengers around in planes. Disney operates theme parks, television networks, movie studios, and retail stores."

"That's it?" Theresa was unimpressed.

"That's it."

"Why do you even have that one in there? I mean, I can't believe any company would need to talk about that."

"You'd be surprised. Some companies don't really agree on whether they're a product or a services company. Others have quiet disagreements about what line of business they should be in, but don't really get into it until they have this conversation during one of our sessions."

"So you make them talk about this for a long time?"

"No. It's generally a five- or ten-minute conversation, sometimes less, sometimes a little more. But it's important to get the definition right before moving on to the other topics."

"Well. That one doesn't seem particularly important for families." Theresa was ready to move on, but then suddenly seemed a little confused.

"Hey, when does Nike decide what kind of shoes to design, and where to sell them, and whether they should use child labor to manufacture them? And when does Southwest Airlines decide whether to fly to Europe or Canada and what kind of prices they're going to charge?"

Rob smiled. "That's the fourth element of clarity."

Before he could start, Nancy entered carrying sandwiches.

"Do you want to take a break?" Rob offered.

"Is Sophia okay? Is she keeping you away from work?" Theresa asked Nancy.

"Not at all. She's a dream."

Theresa looked at the clock. "Let's not take a break. I've got thirty-three minutes left and I think I'm going to need thirty-two and a half of them."

Rob laughed, and erased part of what he had written to give him more space on the whiteboard.

STRATEGY

"Y" ou know, Rob, I have to tell you that as many times as I've heard people talk about strategy, I can't really say I know what the word means."

"You know why that is?"

She shook her head.

"Because no one does."

Theresa looked confused, so Rob explained.

"Everyone uses it differently, even within the same company. Some people think of strategy as a five-year plan, others see it as short-term tactics. Some people confuse strategy with values or marketing slogans."

"What about you guys?"

"Well, Jude likes to say that it's all of those things. And none of them."

"You're going to have to explain that one to me."

Rob looked at the clock. "Okay, but let's just do the *Reader's Digest* version."

He paused while he collected his thoughts.

"The purpose of a strategy is to differentiate a company, but only after you've figured out what your company does, why it does it, and what it stands for." He pointed to the first three items on the board.

"Then you have to figure out how you're going to go about doing it in a way that separates you from your competitors. That way everything the company does, every decision it makes, is done for a reason."

Rob then took some time to provide a number of examples for Theresa, all of which she captured in her notes.

"How do you know when you have the right strategy?"

"You don't." Rob paused. "In fact, there's no such thing."

"How can that be?"

"What I mean is that there's more than one way to skin a cat. The key is to know how you're going to do it and stick to it."

"But aren't there some wrong ways to do it?"

"Oh yeah, you can fail if you completely whiff on your strategy. But the most common problem we find in companies is that they don't really have a strategy at all. They make decisions without anything to guide them, and so they end up with a collection of actions that don't fit together. Before they know what's going on, the company has no direction and is just being reactive and opportunistic, chasing down every new idea without knowing why."

Rob continued. "Part of what we do with our clients is to help them determine what we call their strategic anchors—their three big areas of strategic focus."

64

Theresa was writing feverishly now, but needed to verbalize an insight. "It's kind of like the values. If you try to be everything you end up being nothing. You have to focus on what's most important."

Rob nodded, impressed. "Yeah, I think that's pretty much the key to most of this stuff."

"Would a family have a strategy?"

"I don't know of any that do."

"Isn't that an issue? I mean, you said that the biggest problem with companies is not having one."

Before he could answer, Theresa asked a different question. "Could you apply the principles of a strategy to a family?"

Rob thought about it. "I don't see why not."

And it was at that moment that Theresa felt like she just might be able to make this work at home.

"Okay, what's next?"

GOALS

"What's next is probably the most popular and practically important theory we use with our clients. It's remarkably simple, but it's critical that you understand it."

Theresa looked at the clock on the wall. "Is it simple enough to explain in eleven minutes?"

"I'll give it my best shot."

He paused for a few seconds to plan his line of attack.

"Every organization needs to have a top priority. We call it a 'rallying cry.'"

Theresa nodded her head. "I know this. It's what Jude came up with when he started the firm. But explain it anyway."

"Okay, you've heard the saying, 'If everything's important, nothing is'?"

She wrote it down. "Yeah, Jude says it all the time. Keep going."

"Essentially, that's what having a top priority is all about. Making something most important so that nothing distracts the organization from achieving it. It's about rallying people around one big thing at a time."

"Can you give me an example from one of your clients?"

"Sure. Let's see." He looked out the window as though all the firm's clients were standing in the parking lot waiting to be chosen. "Okay, we worked with a restaurant recently. A regional chain of Italian restaurants on the East Coast."

Theresa raised her hand and waited for Rob to acknowledge her before asking her question. "How many locations did they have?"

Rob frowned in thought. "At the time we worked with them, about thirty, seven of which were considered original stores. And they were planning to grow by adding fifteen more in the Midwest during the following twelve months. Which is why they were so concerned about the drop in same-store revenue, and whether that was an indication that they shouldn't be expanding."

Theresa nodded as if to say *that makes sense,* and Rob continued, writing on the whiteboard as he went.

"They looked under the covers a little and decided that a variety of issues were causing the revenue drop. Turnover among waiters and waitresses had begun to rise, most likely because the decrease in business caused their tips to drop. And that led to increased costs of hiring and training."

Theresa was enjoying the case study. Rob went on.

"Beyond that, the menu hadn't been updated in any meaningful way in almost two years. And some of the neighborhoods where those older stores were located were getting tired and less desirable for suburban customers. And to top it all off, the company had cut back on radio and television advertising slightly."

He paused, and asked Theresa a question. "Now, most executive teams would deal with a situation like this in the same way. Can you guess what that might be?"

Theresa looked at the whiteboard where the four issues were listed, and pondered the question. "I don't know. They all seem pretty important issues to me."

Rob nodded as if to say *that's what they always say,* and asked a different question. "Okay, what would you do if you were in charge?"

She paused, perplexed. "I'd probably try to deal with all of them. I'd change the menu, close restaurants in the worst neighborhoods, find out why people are leaving, and ramp up advertising again."

Rob nodded, as though he were waiting for more.

Theresa smiled uncomfortably. "What?"

Without cracking a smile, Rob asked, "Well, I was just wondering why you wouldn't also hire Celine Dion to be the company spokesperson."

Theresa was a little stunned by the question, then turned sarcastic when she saw Rob smile. "Because I don't like Celine Dion. And she's French Canadian. Billy Joel would be better for an Italian restaurant."

Rob laughed. "You see the problem, though?"

"Well, I guess we wouldn't be able to afford—"

Rob interrupted. "No, it's not just about money. I mean, sure, if you tried to do all of that at once, you'd probably have to spread out your finances so much that you'd do a mediocre job in each area. But even if you could afford to hire Billy Joel and increase advertising and move restaurants out of bad neighborhoods and do everything else you might want to do, it creates a problem because it sends the organization scrambling in different directions."

"I understand that theoretically, but how does that actually look in real life? And shouldn't people be able to do more than one thing at a time?"

"Yes, but only one thing can be most important."

Theresa seemed to be coming along, so Rob kept going.

"Imagine this. The marketing VP starts working with ad agencies to design commercials, not to mention trying to book Celine Dion."

"Billy Joel."

"Right. At the same time, the operations people are out looking for better real estate for the restaurants in the rundown neighborhoods. And the product people are trying new ideas for low carb diets, while the HR folks are piloting a program for increasing salaries for waiters and waitresses in down-market stores."

"What's wrong with that? Isn't that their jobs?"

"Well, it's okay if you're not trying to work as a team. But pretty soon the right hand doesn't know what the left hand is doing. The marketing folks need the new menu

69

items before they can start advertising. The real estate people want extra budget for new construction and improvements, and the VP of HR is trying to convince the CFO that salary adjustments should come first. People are all rowing in different directions and the boat's going nowhere."

"Basically, you're saying they need to have a common—" she hesitated, trying to think of the right word.

Rob said it for her. "A rallying cry."

Theresa didn't raise her hand for the next question. "But how do you know where they should focus or what they should rally around?"

"Well, that's the $64,000 question, isn't it? Assuming, of course, that they have the courage not to try to do everything at once."

"So, did they have the courage?"

"Yeah, eventually we convinced them to take on one issue at a time."

"What issue did they pick?"

"The menu."

"Was that the right one?"

"I don't know."

"Well, did they turn the company around?"

Rob nodded. "Yes, they did."

"So it was the right one."

"Well, I suppose you could say it wasn't the wrong one."

Theresa was suddenly a little exasperated with her instructor. "Aren't you being a little coy here, Rob?"

He smiled, but just a little. "Maybe. But what I'm trying to explain is that what's more important than choosing the right thing is choosing *something*. I mean, sure, you want to make the best decision possible. And the executives at that restaurant chain certainly debated which one would be best. Ultimately, they decided that the menu was at the heart of their business, and that if people weren't excited about the food they offered, changing the other things wouldn't have a large enough impact. But that doesn't mean they couldn't have succeeded if they had chosen better marketing or one of the other priorities."

"You really think so?"

"Absolutely. The best companies don't necessarily make right decisions all the time, but they make clear decisions and get their people rallied around them. Microsoft whiffed on the whole Internet thing, and then changed course and ended up doing better than its competitors who might have been intellectually more accurate, but who couldn't rally their people around the strategy."

Theresa was sold. "Okay, I think goals make sense, and I don't see why a family wouldn't have a rallying cry."

Rob could tell that Theresa was pushing for closure, so he warned her. "Now, there's a lot more to goals after you've chosen your rallying cry. You need to figure out what specific things you need to do to accomplish your big goal. And then you also need to decide on the regular categories that you have to keep your eye on to keep the business running. But that's a longer explanation for another time."

ROLES AND
RESPONSIBILITIES

Theresa looked at the clock. "I'm sorry, but I really have to go. Can you tell me about roles and responsibilities later too?"

"Sure, but that's the easiest one of all. It's just a matter of everyone on the executive team knowing what they have to do when the meeting is over to accomplish whatever it is that they've agreed to do."

Theresa listened as she gathered her notes and purse. "That makes sense. Listen, Rob, I can't tell you how much I appreciate this. I'm ready to burst with ideas, and I hope I can ask you a few follow-up questions and show you what I come up with when I'm done."

"Are you kidding? If you don't, I'll charge you my hourly rate. And Linda will never speak to you again."

"Rob, you are a total sweetheart for doing this. I mean it." Theresa hugged her husband's business partner and left.

As she strapped her daughter into a booster seat and climbed into her minivan, Theresa suddenly had an overwhelming and somewhat depressing thought. Maybe this is all too complicated for a family. But before she could give it any more consideration, her mind shifted to baby-sitters and grocery lists and carpools. Any thoughts about values and strategies and goals quickly receded to the darkest recesses of Theresa's brain.

But they would not stay there for long.

REVIEW

The next day was a little busier than normal for Theresa.

After carpool and swim practice, she went home and made her famous sloppy joes for the kids. She then gave Molly, the teenage babysitter from next door, a few instructions about getting the kids to bed, and went to her school board meeting.

Ninety minutes later, Theresa came home exhausted. Fortunately, the babysitter had managed to get all the kids to sleep, and Theresa had some time to relax and clear her head.

Grabbing a Diet Coke and her notes from the meeting with Rob, she went to the kitchen table and prepared to review the lecture from earlier in the day, just as she had done in college. But before she could start, she heard Jude coming through the front door, a little louder than she would have liked.

After throwing his bags onto the floor, he came into the kitchen looking disheveled and worn.

Theresa looked at the clock. "I didn't expect you until after ten."

"Yeah, the plane was actually early, if you can believe it. And traffic was no problem."

He kissed his wife and dropped himself onto the denim couch in the den, which was adjacent to the kitchen.

Theresa joined him there. "How was Vancouver?"

"Vancouver is beautiful. My client is not. In fact, he's a pain in the butt. But I don't want to talk about him. What's new with you? What did Dr. Robbins have to say yesterday?"

After Theresa explained the situation, Jude changed subjects.

"And what about your session with Rob? Did you already know all the stuff he went over?"

Theresa shook her head. "Absolutely not. I remembered some of it, but it's been quite a while since I had my head in your work. So his lecture was helpful."

Jude was surprised by her muted answer. "That's it? Helpful?"

"Well, Rob was wonderful, as usual. And I thought it was very interesting. It's just I'm a little confused."

She hesitated, but sensing that her husband was genuinely eager to hear what she had to say, continued. "What exactly were you thinking when you said that your clients would go out of business if they ran their companies like our family?"

Because he was tired, Jude was a little defensive now. "Listen, I never should have said that. But I've apologized at least three times and I think you could let up—"

Theresa interrupted. "No, I'm not complaining. It's just that it would be helpful to know what was going through your mind at the time you said it."

Jude took a breath and changed his disposition. "Well, to tell you the truth, Theresa, I don't think I gave it all that much thought. I guess I was just thinking that we're a little disorganized."

"Disorganized? Is that really it?"

Jude put his head back on the couch and stared at the ceiling as though his memory were somehow displayed there. "Yeah, I think so. It was really just an expression."

"Well, that's disappointing."

Jude smiled, trying to decide whether he should be amused or annoyed. "Why do you say that?"

"Because I was hoping that you had come to the same conclusion that I came to earlier tonight."

"Earlier tonight?"

"Yeah, at the school board meeting."

Suddenly Jude remembered his schedule conflict. "Oh, crap! I hope you told them that I was out of town and that my calendar was double-booked."

Theresa patted him on the shoulder. "Yes, I did. And they were completely understanding. Mrs. Hourigan wasn't even there, and without the principal, we wouldn't have been able to do your strategic planning overview anyway."

Jude was relieved.

Theresa continued. "But we did talk about the idea of

clarifying our mission and our values. And that's when I had my epiphany."

"I'm all ears."

"Well, I realized that the school is putting together a plan, and I know that the church did it last year, and most of the companies in the world do, right?"

He nodded. "Right."

"So why don't families?"

Jude looked like he had been asked why champagne didn't run from the kitchen faucet. "I don't know. I guess it's because," he hesitated, "we're a family and not a business or an organization."

"Why are we not an organization?"

Jude raised his eyebrows as he pondered her question. "Well, I guess because we. . . . " He hesitated long enough for Theresa to interrupt.

"You don't have an answer, do you?"

Jude smiled and shook his head. "Not a clue. I don't know why we don't think of families as organizations. In fact, it makes no sense at all."

Theresa was buoyed by her husband's admission. "But there must be a reason."

Jude looked back at the ceiling for another elusive answer. After a full five seconds of consideration he replied, "I think it's probably because we're lazy. We like the idea that we can just live our home lives by the seats of our pants, without any real cost."

"Don't you think there's a cost?"

"Sure, but it's not a very tangible one. And no one gets fired for doing a lousy job."

Suddenly it occurred to Jude that it might have sounded like he was criticizing his wife again. He moved quickly to clarify. "That's not directed at you. Because I'm not saying that you're doing a lousy job. I'm just thinking about the fact that there is no real planning. And that's not your responsibility alone. It's both of ours. Or any couple's."

Theresa laughed. "Relax, I'm not going to tear into you again. But I appreciate the clarification."

Jude let out his breath in relief, and continued. "I do think your point is a good one, though. I wouldn't let the smallest client of mine get away with managing their business without a plan, and yet most parents just wing it when it comes to managing their families."

"So you think this is the norm?"

"Well, I've certainly never met anyone who had a real family plan. I mean, I suppose it's possible, but you'd think we'd have heard about it by now. The most organized people I know get by with a computer and a whiteboard with a calendar on it, but that hardly constitutes a purposeful approach to domestic management."

Theresa was starting to get excited. "So let's do it."

Jude was tempted to make a joke about getting frisky, but didn't want to diminish the moment. "Sounds great. When?"

Theresa looked at the clock. "Well, I'm free for the next two hours."

"Now?" Jude laughed. "I was thinking we could watch some TV and go to bed."

Theresa shook her head. "Sorry, buddy. It's time to get to work."

Jude stared at his wife in amused disbelief. "All right, then."

LATE NIGHTER

Jude grabbed his laptop and a fistful of Red Vines from the pantry and headed for the kitchen table, where his wife had already spread out her notes.

Theresa was going to drive the conversation. "Where would you usually start with one of your clients?"

"Well, it depends on the client. What industry they're in and how big they are."

"So what do you think?" Theresa asked.

"We probably ought to think about a fairly small company. Although now that I think about it, it doesn't really matter that much. We use mostly the same approach for all our clients."

Theresa had her notebook in front of her. "Ready when you are."

Jude began. "Okay, it's pretty straightforward. We would usually begin by asking them about the reason the company was initially started. . . ."

Theresa dove in. "Right, beyond making money. The core purpose."

Jude was impressed. "Wow, Rob must have been a good teacher."

"Nope," she stated in mock protest. "I'm a good student."

Theresa smiled and kept driving. "Do you think core purpose is relevant to families? Or is it pretty much the same from one family to another?"

Jude considered the question. "It's definitely relevant. And no, I don't think it's exactly the same from one family to another. But," he hesitated, "I don't know. It might be a little overkill to actually spell it out. But then again," he paused again in indecision, "I don't know. What do you think?"

"I think we should try to come up with one for our family, and see if it helps."

For the next twenty minutes Theresa and Jude discussed and debated why they had started their family and what their ultimate purpose was. They vacillated between overly tactical statements like "to clothe, feed, and educate our children" to overly vague ones like "to make the world a better place." Finally, they arrived at a statement that reflected the importance of family and children within the context of their faith.

Theresa and Jude read it a few times and decided that their purpose statement was a good one. But she wasn't sure exactly how they would use it, and she was eager to move on to talk about values.

FAMILY VALUES

Theresa had been looking forward to the next conversation ever since Rob's lecture.

"I have an idea," she announced. "Let's each take a stab at identifying what our core values ought to be, and see how close we are."

Jude was a little hesitant. "Well, it might be better if we talk about core values first so we don't mix them up with the other kinds and end up with a list a half-mile long."

"You mean aspirational, accidental and," she looked at her notes, "'permission-to-play'?"

Jude was impressed. "Wow, you are a good student!"

Theresa smiled. "No—Rob's a good teacher."

The parents dove into their individual exercises, Jude moving into the living room to think, Theresa staying in the kitchen. Just ten minutes later they were back at the table ready to compare notes.

Theresa asked Jude to go first.

"Okay, I have four words here. I don't know if they're the right words, but I think they get at the concepts I'm trying to convey. They are *excellence, humility, passion,* and," he paused, "the word I used is *empathy,* but I don't know if that's exactly right. What did you come up with?"

Theresa was excited. "I also had *passion.*"

Jude raised his eyebrows to acknowledge that they had both identified one of the same values. "Interesting."

Theresa smiled. "That's not all. I also have *humility.*"

Jude's eyes went even wider now. "No way."

Theresa explained her choice of humility. "I just hate it when people brag. I always have, and that's one of the things I love about you. You always deflect attention away from yourself. Maybe to a fault, but I love it anyway."

Jude had an epiphany. "That's funny that you say 'to a fault'—because one of the things about core values is that an organization will often take them to an extreme that's not always helpful, but that's what makes it core—they do it anyway. And that's part of the deal, taking the good with the occasional bad."

Theresa was taking notes again now. "Ooh, Rob didn't explain that to me. Can you give me an example from the business world?"

"Sure. Let's see." He looked down into his lap as though he were reading from a cheat sheet, except his eyes were closed. "I always use Southwest Airlines as an example here."

"Yeah, why do you talk about them so much?"

"Because they're just so darn good at core values, and most things for that matter. But especially when it comes to values. See, one of their values is humor. They call it 'having a fun-loving spirit.' And as you know, that means they make jokes a lot on flights, even during the boring and serious safety instructions flight attendants do before the plane takes off."

Theresa nodded her head. "Yeah, I once heard a guy say, 'In the event of a water landing, we'll be coming by your seat with drinks and towels.'"

Jude laughed. "Exactly. It's not that they don't do the safety instructions, or that they don't care about safety. They just try to make it fun, for passengers and employees alike."

Theresa was writing again.

Jude continued his story. "Well, one day a woman, who was a long-time customer, wrote a letter to the CEO of Southwest, complaining about the humor, especially in serious matters like safety. Now, most companies would have sent that customer a nice note saying 'we're sorry' and 'we value you as a customer' and 'we'll look into this and do our best to make sure it doesn't happen again.'"

Theresa smiled. "What did Southwest do?"

The look on Jude's face said *you're not going to believe this*. "Rumor has it that the CEO sent her a letter with three words on it. 'We'll miss you.'"

Theresa howled with laughter. "I love it!" She paused for a moment. "But I'm not sure that's such a good idea. Why not try to keep her as a customer?"

"That's the thing about a core value. You never abandon it, even if some people don't like that about you, or even if it's inconvenient. How can they tell their new hires that humor is important, and encourage them to incorporate humor in just about everything they do, and then tell them to rein it in every time a customer decides it's not in good taste? They're going to kill the goose that lays the golden eggs."

Theresa started writing again.

Jude pressed on. "Okay, let's hear your other values."

"Oh, right. Let's see." She turned back to the page where she had written them. "Like I said, I have *passion* and *humility,* and I can't believe you had those exact same words too. I also have *self-control, compassion,* and *respect.*"

Jude frowned.

"What's wrong?" Theresa sounded like a fourth grader who just learned that she'd misspelled a word on a test.

"Nothing. It's just that *respect* seems a little generic to me. I'm not sure that shouldn't be a—"

"Permission-to-play value?"

Again, Jude was impressed. "Yeah, probably. And the other one that I'm struggling with is *self-control.*" He tried to keep himself from smiling, but couldn't.

Theresa laughed. "What are you saying? Because I'm not the poster child for self-control. Are you stereotyping me because I'm Italian?"

He laughed too. "Well, I'm just saying that I think self-control might be an aspirational value. I wouldn't consider it to be one of my strengths, either."

Theresa agreed. "What about compassion?"

Jude thought about it. "You know, I think that's core to what we believe and what we're teaching the kids. And it's different from passion, because it's about people."

Theresa was glad that he understood where she was coming from.

For the next few minutes the leaders of the Cousins family refined their list and settled on *passion, humility,* and *compassion.* Theresa typed those words immediately beneath the Core Purpose statement they had settled on earlier.

As Theresa sat and looked at those simple words and sentences typed on Jude's computer, she felt a sense of accomplishment and relief that she and Jude had described something important and real, something that might guide them as parents for the rest of their lives.

Unfortunately, she still didn't know exactly how that was going to happen.

ATTRITION

Jude looked at the clock and yawned. "Wow, it's past midnight and I'm wiped out. Can we pick this up tomorrow night?"

Theresa squinted, reviewing the calendar in her head. "Tomorrow night. Let's see. We have back-to-school night. Which reminds me that I have to get another babysitter. Wow, we're paying a fortune in babysitting this month."

Jude's financial warning alarm would normally have been set off by a statement like that, but he was just too tired. "Okay, let's go to Starbucks for an hour after back-to-school night, and we can do more of this then."

Theresa slowly nodded. "All right. But I think I'm going to stay up and work on it a little longer, if that's okay. That way I'll have something to show you tomorrow night."

"Fine with me." He stood, kissed his wife on the forehead, and left the room.

Theresa found another Diet Coke in the back of the fridge and went back to the kitchen table. It was time to take on strategy.

SLEEP HANGOVER

When Jude woke up the next morning to go for an early run, he noticed that the kitchen table was still covered with Theresa's papers from the night before, and that his laptop was still on.

I wonder how late she was up.

When he came home sweaty from his three-mile workout, he found out.

"Three-thirty," Theresa explained, a little embarrassed and more than a little exhausted. "But I think I got a lot done."

After she got the twins and Sophia out the door for carpool, and had Michael fed and parked in front of the television watching one of the Baby Einstein videos, Theresa offered to show Jude the product of her late-night work.

"If you have a second, here's what I came up with for strategy."

"I'm sorry, I've got to leave here in fifteen minutes, and I still have to shower and shave. But we have a date tonight after back-to-school night, right?"

Theresa excused her husband and started to clean the kitchen and begin her daily routine.

By the time evening rolled around, Theresa was feeling the effects of having burned the midnight oil, but she was glad to be going out on a date with her husband, even if it was just back-to-school night at St. Anthony's elementary.

Because they had three girls at St. Anthony's, Jude and Theresa split up to cover each one of the classrooms. After an hour of presentations and conversations, they headed for Starbucks. On the way, Theresa shared some news about one of their daughters that concerned her.

"Mrs. Schroeder said that Emily was crying at lunch yesterday."

"What about?"

"She didn't know. By the time she asked, Emily seemed fine and didn't want to talk about it."

"Well, that's pretty normal for a nine-year-old girl to cry once in a while, isn't it?"

"Mrs. Schroeder said it was the third time. And they've only been in school for two weeks."

Jude frowned. "Well, we'll just have to talk to her."

"I think I know what it's about," Theresa confessed.

SUBURBAN DILEMMA

"Soccer?" Jude was puzzled. "Why would she be crying about soccer?"

"It's the all-star thing. She feels bad because she's not on the team."

"But I thought she decided she didn't want to be on the team."

"She did, but that's just because she doesn't want to play all year round, and because Hailey probably wouldn't have made it. She really wants to play with Hailey."

"That sounds like a good decision to me."

"To me too, but the girls in her class who are on the all-star team have been a little petty about it. They don't pick Emily for their team at recess. I know that sounds silly, but—"

Jude interrupted. "No, I remember fourth grade. That kind of stuff stinks." He paused. "Do you think we should've encouraged her to play on the all-star team?"

"No," she announced confidently, then hesitated. "I don't think so. Do you?"

Jude sighed. "I don't know. I mean, it's crazy that a nine-year-old little girl would be asked to play soccer ten months of the year, and wouldn't even be on her sister's team. But then I hear these crazy soccer parents say that if they don't play on the all-star team by age eleven, they'll never have a chance to play high school soccer."

Theresa was incredulous. "That's just plain stupid. Who makes these rules?"

"It's not a rule, it's just a matter of living in an ultra-competitive area."

"What's the point, anyway? Do these people think their daughters are going to play on the Olympic team?"

"World Cup, honey."

"Whatever. Do they think soccer is going to be their life?"

Jude shook his head in mild disgust. "I don't know. I suppose they're hoping for a college scholarship, or maybe just want to live out their sports fantasies through their kids. But then again, who are we to judge? If that's what they want. . . . " He didn't finish the sentence.

"They can have it, if you ask me." She paused for a few seconds while Jude drove. "The sad thing is that Emily is really good, and it's a shame that she might be aced out just because we don't let her dedicate her life to a sport before she wears a bra."

Jude agreed. "You know, it's almost as though you have to make a decision between playing high-level competitive sports and having a normal family. When we were kids, you could do both."

Theresa took a deep breath and looked out her window at the passing neighborhood. After a full thirty seconds of silence, she finally spoke. "Let's move, Jude."

He answered before he realized the magnitude of her question. "Move where?"

"I don't know. Somewhere slower. Somewhere simpler. This is not how I envisioned life. Is this how you thought it would be?"

He paused. "No. I guess not." He thought for a few seconds. "But I just can't see us pulling up stakes and moving." Another pause. "Are you serious?"

"Yeah, I think so. I don't know."

They arrived at the coffee shop and allowed themselves to postpone their weighty conversation.

While standing in line, Theresa shifted gears and attempted to set the stage for the meeting they had gone there to have. "Okay, one of the things I want to do tonight is go over the three anchors of our strategy. Or at least what I think they are."

Jude seemed hesitant. "Did Rob take enough time to really explain the concept of strategy?"

Theresa nodded. "Yeah, and I think I get it. But you can tell me if I'm doing it wrong."

As they came to the counter to order, they suddenly saw a few of the other parents from Hailey and Emily's classes enter the store. After waving and making small talk, they ordered their usual exotic beverages, with Jude asking for a medium just to make the cashier correct him and say "grande." Two minutes later they retrieved their orders and found a table in a somewhat remote corner of the room. As always, the temperature inside the place was freezing.

Realizing the limited time they had, Jude got things moving. "Okay, tell me what you think our strategic anchors are."

FAMILY STRATEGY

Theresa was a little hesitant, but mostly excited, about sharing the results of her work from the previous night. "Now this is just my first guess, but I think that anchor number one is 'Mom Stays Home.'"

Jude thought about it for a few seconds as he burned his tongue on a chai tea latte.

Theresa sensed that he was skeptical. "You don't think that's right?"

He shook his head. "No, it's definitely in the right area, and it may be right. It's just, well, maybe your staying home is really in service of something bigger."

"I don't understand."

"Well, why do you stay home from work? What is the larger reason?"

She didn't have to think long. "We decided we wanted to spend a lot of time with our kids. But everyone wants that?"

"Yes, but not to the same extent. I mean, we always said we wanted to find every way possible to give our kids

94

every ounce of spare time we have, without crowding them or making us insane."

Theresa nodded. "Yeah, I remember those conversations."

"So that's why you stay home. And it's why I don't take on clients overseas. We don't want me to be gone too much so we can be involved in the kids' lives."

Theresa was writing this down and nodding. "And it's why we both coach soccer, even though it's a pain in the butt to bring Michael with me to practice every Thursday." She paused and looked up. "So, what would you call that?"

Jude thought about it. "It doesn't really matter what we call it, as long as we know what it means. But if you want to name it something, how about," he paused, "quantity time?"

"Quantity time?"

"Yeah, you know how people talk about quality time. Well, we're doing *quantity* time."

She laughed. "That sounds like we don't care about whether the time we spend with the kids is meaningful."

"No, it's just that we're going to place our bets on maximizing our involvement in their lives."

Theresa looked around the coffee shop and frowned. "I don't know."

"What's the problem?"

"Doesn't this make us sound like we're being judgmental about families where the moms work? How would your sister feel about hearing this?" Jude's younger sister and her husband were both doctors, and relied on all-day day care for their two boys.

Jude's eyebrows went up, as if to say *where did that come from?* "Well, first of all, no one needs to know our strategy but us. We don't market or advertise it. But more important, it's up to us to live the way we think is best for our kids and our family. To be purposeful about it all. If someone disagrees with us or chooses a different way, that's up to them. We're not trying to make a statement here, just to get clarity about how we manage our family."

Theresa understood. "I know. It's just there's a lot of pressure out there for moms."

"I know. We deal with it at work too. But some families can't afford to live in a good neighborhood or go to good schools if both parents don't work. That's their reality and the decision they make. Other people work part-time because they need more income so they go on really nice vacations. Others just don't want to stay home because they'd get bored."

"Of course they get bored!"

Jude laughed. "Whoa, Nellie. No need to get excited."

"Sorry, it's just that if people think staying home isn't boring sometimes. . . . "

She didn't finish the sentence, so Jude continued.

"Anyway, the point here isn't so much about what you decide, it's about making a decision and using it. Otherwise you're just flailing."

Suddenly Theresa bolted up as though something struck a chord with her. "That's exactly what it feels like! Flailing! Every decision is like reinventing the wheel. Should we go on vacation with the Harrisons? Should we move into a bigger house? Teach the kids to ski? Talk to them about sex? Adopt a baby? Buy organic groceries? Let Sophia watch *SpongeBob?* It's overwhelming!" Theresa started to laugh. And for a split second it looked like she was about to cry.

"What's wrong?"

"Nothing. I think it's just the lack of sleep after last night."

But Jude knew it was more than that.

BAD TIMING

As Theresa pulled herself together, someone interrupted their conversation. "Hey there, you guys! I didn't see you sitting over here."

It was Candace Barrington, the mother of one of Hailey and Emily's classmates.

"I tried to find you tonight at school because I wanted to talk to you about something." She didn't pause long enough to let them ask any questions. "Do you think we can carpool for all-star soccer? If I have to drive Carrie out there three times a week, I'm going to go crazy."

Jude smiled at Theresa and nodded as if to say, *why don't you take this one.*

Theresa cleared her throat. "Well, the girls aren't playing all-star soccer."

Candace was stunned. "Really. Emily's not on the team? She was one of the best players in the Pony League last year."

"Well, she wants to play with her sister, and we're just not ready for such a commitment."

The woman winced. "You know, it's going to be harder for her to get on that team next year. I mean, if the coaches and trainers don't know her."

Jude entered the conversation now. "Yeah, that's okay. We'll have a good time in Pony again. She's got plenty of years for sports ahead of her, but time with her sister is kind of precious right now."

Candace responded emphatically but without sincerity. "Of course it is. These are just little girls after all." She paused. "Well, I've to get home. It's great seeing you guys."

They said their good-byes, and as soon as Candace was out of the store and out of sight, Jude and Theresa started laughing.

"Can you believe that?" Theresa shook her head. "Right on cue. That's the kind of thing that drives me crazy."

Jude wanted to distract his wife from Candace and what she represented. "Let's get back to work."

For the next twenty minutes, the couple discussed and massaged what they thought would be their other two strategic anchors. First, they settled on what Theresa called "Faith and Church."

"After all," Theresa explained, "we both volunteer at church, send our kids to school there, and a lot of our friends come from there. Between Bible study and carpool and Mass on Sundays and school board, it's like a second home. Which I love."

Jude agreed.

It didn't take them long to agree that the other anchor probably had something to do with staying physically active, though their decisiveness on that issue had more to do with their eagerness to move on to goals than anything else.

RALLY

"**S**o what do you think our rallying cry ought to be?" Jude wanted to know. He was enjoying this far more than he'd thought he would.

Theresa hesitated. "The rallying cry is the big goal, right?"

Jude nodded.

"Well, I think it's about what we're doing here tonight, getting our heads and hands around family clarity."

Jude winced.

"What's the problem with that?" Theresa wanted to know.

"Well, it's just that it seems more like a first step, and not really a family rallying cry."

Theresa looked a little disappointed, so Jude explained his rationale. "Don't get me wrong. I think this is all critical and necessary, and we'll never move forward if we don't do it. It just doesn't match up to a rallying cry, which should take somewhere between two and six months to accomplish. We can have this one done in two days."

Theresa wrote that down. "Rob didn't explain that part. Anyway, I'm guessing you have an idea of what a better rallying cry might be."

"Not really. But I think it's probably related to the reason that you feel the need to do all this in the first place. The question you need to ask is, 'What is it that you want to be different in our lives six months from now?'"

Theresa's eyes lit up. "Well, if you ask it that way, the answer's easy."

Jude waited for her to tell him.

"We need to spend more time together as a family."

Jude was about to ask a question, but Theresa already knew what he was thinking. "Yes, I realize that we probably spend more time together than most families. But I'm talking about the whole family being together, and without any activities. At home. Playing games. Watching movies. Reading. Playing. Just being together."

Jude considered it and began to nod slowly. "That's more along the lines of what we talked about when we got married. Somehow now it seems like a pipe dream."

"That's the thing, Jude. I don't think it has to be. If we can just find a way to stop reacting to every request to join a committee or have someone over for a sleepover or to sign up for every sport that the neighbors sign up for or go on vacation to the same places that everyone else goes to. The time we have as a family is short, and it's just too important to let the rest of the world dictate how we're going to live it."

At that moment, Jude looked at his watch. "Ooh, you know what else is important? Getting home. We told Charlotte we'd be there by eight-thirty, and we've got approximately fifteen seconds or we'll be late."

COLD WATER

As they drove home, Theresa was quiet.

Jude thought out loud. "I hope Charlotte isn't mad." Charlotte was their beloved long-time babysitter, and because she was always so accommodating, they never wanted to take advantage of her.

Theresa didn't respond, but after a moment, she started to cry softly.

Jude usually tried to use humor in these situations to avoid an emotional conversation. "Oh, she won't be that mad. And I'll let you sneak in the back door so you don't have to see her."

Theresa didn't react to the lame joke.

Jude had no choice now. He put his hand on his wife's shoulder. "What's wrong, honey?"

After a few more sniffles, she explained. "Oh, I'm just afraid to get old, I think."

Jude smiled. "Hey, everyone turns forty. It's the new thirty."

"I'm not thinking about forty. It's fifty I'm worried about."

"Fifty? Don't you think you're getting a little ahead of yourself?"

"No. I mean, I don't want to spend another decade flailing and find myself at fifty, stressed out and just surviving. If this clarity thing doesn't work out, Jude," she said, fighting back her tears, "then I honestly think we should move. Really, I do."

At that moment Jude realized just how serious Theresa's quest for sanity and clarity was, and that it would have to become his quest too.

PART THREE

Trial and Error

DOCUMENTATION

That night, Theresa typed up a document called "Cousins Family Clarity" and printed a copy. She three-hole punched it, slipped it into a binder, and put a cover page on it with the same name. With a sense of satisfaction, relief, and exhaustion, she put the binder on the shelf above her desk in the kitchen and went to bed.

The next few days were particularly busy, with Jude out of town one night and the girls starting to bring home more homework than they were used to. The weekend was filled with one of the first soccer tournaments of the year, which meant four games spread across two fields in different parts of town. Add church and an unexpected visit from Jude's sister to the mix, and by Sunday night Theresa was too tired and overwhelmed to even consider "the big picture," as she liked to call it.

The next week was no calmer, and it included appointments with the allergy doctor as well as a baby shower for a friend. Theresa was always amazed at how just two irregular events in a week filled any free time she had hoped to use for projects at home.

Soon enough, Theresa was back in the survival groove, trying to stay ahead of the daily schedule and get a little free time to watch an hour of TV with Jude. At times she would try to convince herself that she had overreacted, that the life she was living was inevitable, and that she could manage getting by like this for another ten or fifteen years.

But every night she went to bed with a subtle but undeniable sense that she was failing, that there was a good chance she would never put her plan to work, and that moving was looking better and better.

GOING PUBLIC

Theresa woke the next morning in something of a panic, determined to put her dormant discoveries into practice. Deciding that a good way to increase her chances would be to share it with others, she invited a handful of friends for lunch later in the week to learn her new system.

Of course, she had to invite Kelly Horan and Alison Marsh, given their initial conversations. And Linda couldn't be excluded either. Wanting to ensure that her test group had some families of different sizes and situations, she also invited Danielle Knox, a childhood friend who lived in San Francisco and worked full-time as a lawyer, and Jude's older sister Jan, a widow raising two children on her own. With her youngest child in high school, Jan had recently returned to work as a behavioral therapist in the school system.

To Theresa's delight, every invitee not only agreed to come but seemed genuinely interested in what Theresa had explained in her e-mail invitation. The meeting would not be a disappointment. At least not initially.

LUNCH MEETING

Desperately coaxing Michael into an early nap, Theresa prepared her home and her mind for her experimental group.

After the customary twenty minutes of introductions and socializing and catching up, the visitors sat down to eat lunch and listen to their friend's scheduled presentation. Though she knew each of the women fairly well and was comfortable with them on an individual basis, Theresa was surprised to find herself somewhat nervous now that she was actually speaking to them as a group. Luckily, she found that her attack of nerves dissipated quickly.

Theresa started by explaining how her "project" came about, including Jude's infamous remark about clients. She then told them about the lecture that Rob had delivered, and her subsequent conversations with Jude. Finally, she presented the six elements of organizational clarity, followed by a brief overview of the first draft of the Cousins Family Plan.

The response from the group could not have been better. There were plenty of questions and comments and enthusiastic laughter about the frantic states of their respective families. And it was clear that each of them would have different answers for the questions Theresa put before them.

After a little more than an hour, the eclectic collection of moms left the Cousins house excited about discussing the ideas with their husbands and putting them to work in their homes. Or so Theresa thought.

STASIS

That night Theresa reported the success of her meeting to Jude, who was relieved to see the return of his wife's normal enthusiasm. Unfortunately, over the next week he saw that enthusiasm begin to fade when none of Theresa's friends called to report any progress.

One morning, as she fed Michael while Jude ate cereal, Theresa vented to her husband. "I'm really surprised that I haven't heard from any of them yet."

"It's only been a week."

"Yeah, but you'd think that just one of them would have called by now."

"I thought you said Linda did."

"She called to say thank you, but not to tell me how it was going for her and Rob."

"Listen, they're busy. This takes awhile. And if they haven't gotten around to it, they're probably feeling a little guilty. Remember when Nora Galvez tried to get us to go on that retreat, and we were always avoiding her out of guilt because we weren't ready to commit? Give them time."

"I guess I'm just not in a very patient mood right now, Jude." Almost on cue, Michael proceeded to dump a container of peaches onto the floor.

Jude got up to clean the mess, without missing a beat. "Well, you can always call them yourself."

"No, I don't want to seem pushy. I'll give it more time."

"What about us?"

"What do you mean?"

"How are we doing on our strategic plan?"

"Between the girls being sick and the time I spent getting ready for the session with my friends, I haven't quite had time to finish putting the plan in place. But it's just a matter of sitting down for a half hour one of these days."

Jude thought about pushing back on her for her own procrastination, but decided against it. Besides, he was doing his best not to get peaches on his slacks.

Two weeks later, he'd wish he had pushed his wife a little harder.

IMPATIENCE

After another week without hearing from her friends, Theresa decided to swallow her pride and call them. She wasn't prepared for the disappointment she was about to experience.

Alison Marsh's response was pretty typical. "I talked to Scott about it the night of our lunch, but when I tried to explain the five or six areas that we talked about at your house, I got a little stuck. Since then I've been swamped with two baby showers and getting ready for a big speech tournament next week. I'm going to try to pick it up again in the next few weeks."

Surprisingly, Linda Groninger was the most direct, if not flippant, of all. "Listen, dear, I think it's just too much. I don't have the time or energy to get my head wrapped around so much stuff. Trying to understand the difference between strategy and values and goals and purpose and profit and whatever. It's beyond me, I'm afraid."

Though she did her best to hide her disappointment from her friends, inside Theresa was frustrated with them.

That night before bed, she complained to Jude. "I can't believe that they didn't even try. I mean, it's not rocket science."

Jude gently reminded his wife, "Don't forget that you had an individual lesson with Rob, then you and I spent some time working on this. You can't expect them to completely understand it in one shot."

"Yeah, but it's almost like they don't think they're capable of understanding it."

"Well, that sounds a little like you when Rob said he'd explain these concepts to you. Diving back into this stuff after being out of it for a while is a little intimidating."

Theresa shook her head. "Maybe, but what about Danielle. She's a lawyer. She isn't out of practice. She isn't using it either."

"Maybe Linda's right."

"What do you mean?"

"Well, you said she thought it was too complex. Maybe it needs to be simpler."

Theresa thought about it. "Is it too complex for your clients?"

Jude raised his eyebrows. "Well, it might be if we only had an hour to describe it to them. But we spend two days going over it, and then we're available to help them later and answer questions if they get stuck. Which is more often than not. And since they pay us plenty of money, they have an incentive to figure it out. That's not how it is when you're running a family."

Theresa slowly shook her head in disappointment as she considered her husband's comment.

Jude continued. "Now, I have a difficult question for you. And it's not meant to make you feel guilty, but I need you to be honest, and maybe even a little tough on yourself." He paused. "Can you tell me why you haven't been using our plan more?"

She looked at Jude directly in the eyes and squinted, as though she was trying to read his mind. Finally, she said three words:

"It's too much."

When Jude didn't say anything, she took a deep breath and went on. "It needs to be simpler and easier." She paused again. "You're right. They're right. Crap."

She gathered up her papers in frustration.

"You're not going to throw in the towel, are you?"

"Are you kidding? I'm going to figure out how to make this simpler."

"Let me know if you need any help."

"Oh, I will."

Theresa kissed her husband good night and left with her papers in hand. Normally Jude would have encouraged her to go to bed and get some rest, but he knew she needed to work this out. It was a good decision on his part.

ALARM

"Wake up, Jude. I need to talk to you."

Jude rolled over and looked at the clock next to his bed. It was 2:38.

"Is something wrong?"

Theresa was smiling. "I think I figured it out."

"Figured what out?"

"How to simplify the model. I think I figured it out."

Jude sat up in bed. "Do I have any chance of talking you out of this conversation right now?"

"Absolutely none. Come on."

Jude followed his bouncing wife out the door to the kitchen.

By the time he arrived, Theresa was already sitting at the table, which was cluttered with papers, Jude's computer, and two Diet Coke cans.

Looking at the computer screen, she began. "Okay, I think I figured it out."

"Yeah, I think you told me that."

"Sorry, it's just I'm kind of excited, and I'm a little worried it's that my judgment is impaired because of all the caffeine, aspartame, and exhaustion."

For precisely those reasons, Jude's expectations were low. Through a yawn he said, "Fire away, sweetheart."

"I've gone back through all of the clarity stuff, the values and purpose and strategy and goals and business definition and whatever else was in there. I've thrown some things out and combined a few others." She paused and looked at him. "Basically, I've boiled it down to the two questions a family has to answer about itself."

Jude rubbed his eyes. "I'm still listening."

"First question: What makes your family unique or different from every other family on the block?"

Jude took it in but didn't really react, so Theresa went on.

"Second question: What is the top priority, the one thing that is most important in your family right now?"

"How do you answer the first question? Is it values or strategy or core purpose?"

She smiled. "Yes."

"Excuse me?"

"All of them. Any of them. It doesn't really matter. What's important is just that you know what makes your family unique."

Jude seemed a little skeptical. "So what would that be for our family then?"

She looked through her notes. "We're a large, close family where the parents are immersed in the lives of their children. The family's life is centered around church and faith, and we believe in being passionate and emotionally invested in everything we do."

"That sounds more like a paragraph than a list of things."

Theresa nodded. "Exactly. And that's okay. It's a lot easier for people to just describe what's unique about their family in their own words, rather than trying to fit it into neat categories."

"But you still would want to talk about values and strategy and purpose, right?"

Theresa thought about it. "Yeah, I think you'd have to. But you don't need to worry about which category your answer fits into. All you have to do is make sure that your answer is true, and that it isn't something that every other family on your street would say too."

Jude frowned. "I don't know. There's a difference between a value and a strategic anchor. Values don't really change over time, and strategies do."

"Yeah, that's what Rob said. But you know, a group of executives might have the time and the energy to split those hairs. But for most families, just knowing what makes them unique is enough."

Jude conceded. "I suppose you don't want to make the perfect the enemy of the good."

"Say that again."

"Don't make the perfect the enemy of the good. It means—"

Theresa interrupted. "Yeah, I think I know what it means. And that's exactly right. Families aren't going to take three hours to figure out the difference between strategy and values. They just need to get some messy clarity out there and use it. And all they need to do is answer two questions."

Jude still seemed just a bit skeptical and was about to make a comment. But before he could, Theresa cut him off. "Before you say anything, consulting boy, remember that families are different from businesses. You know businesses better than I do. But I think I know families better."

He stopped. "You're right. I'm too deep into the business stuff. The fact is, if every family knew what made them unique and what their rallying cry was, they'd be exponentially clearer and more focused."

"Exactly. But there is one thing that still bothers me a little." She didn't wait for her husband to ask. "I'd think that families would need a little more structure around how to go about rallying around their big goal. Just calling it out doesn't seem like enough when there are so many competing priorities."

"You're absolutely correct. Didn't Rob explain the idea of defining objectives and standard objectives?"

Theresa tried to recall the specifics of his lecture that seemed to have taken place so long ago. "You know, he did say something about going into more detail during another conversation. Maybe that's what he meant."

"I'm sure it's what he meant."

"Can you explain it to me? Or maybe I should have Rob do it."

Jude looked her straight in the eye. "Listen, you don't wake a guy up at two thirty-eight in the morning and then tell him you don't need his help."

She smiled. "You're right. You can explain it to me. How long will it take?"

"Fifteen minutes. Twenty, tops."

"I'll make some coffee."

NUTS AND BOLTS

hen Theresa returned to the table after setting up the coffee maker, Jude had moved his computer to the side and was working with a blank sheet of paper.

"Okay, this is not at all complicated, but it's one of the most powerful things we do for our clients, if not the most powerful. It's all about defining the specifics beneath the rallying cry."

She nodded.

"So what's our thematic goal again?"

"You've already forgotten?"

"At this hour, I've forgotten my middle name."

She laughed. "Okay, okay. It's *spend more 'quantity time' together as a family.*"

"That's right." He remembered, and wrote it at the top of the paper and drew a box around it.

```
┌─────────────────────────────────┐
│   Spend more "quantity time"     │
│     together as a family         │
└─────────────────────────────────┘
```

"Okay. What would we have to do to make this a reality?"

Theresa thought about it. "I don't know. Maybe measure exactly how much time we need to spend together?" It was a question more than a guess.

Jude shook his head. "Nope. It's not about measurements or metrics. It's much simpler than that."

She shrugged. "I don't know."

"Let me ask the question in a different way. What would have to be true in order for us to say that we'd accomplished this?"

Theresa frowned in thought. "Well, we'd have to cut back on extracurricular activities, for sure."

He nodded and wrote that in a smaller box beneath the rallying cry. "By the way, we call these 'defining objectives' because they define what is required to do the rallying cry."

She wrote that down.

> Spend more "quantity time"
> together as a family

> Cut back on
> extracurricular
> activities

Jude continued. "Okay, what else? What would the other defining objectives be?"

She thought about it for a few seconds. "I hate to say this, but we'd probably have to cut back on some of the social activities too. We probably need to do a little less with other families, and more with just the six of us."

He nodded and made a face as if to say *that's a good one* and wrote it in another box.

"What else?"

"How many should there be?"

"As many as there need to be, but for some reason, it usually turns out to be four or five."

After a few more seconds of thought, she was suddenly excited. "Oh, I know. We'd have to watch less television. Not just the kids, but you and me too."

"Ouch," Jude joked. "Another good one." He wrote it down.

Theresa got up to attend to the coffee. "Can you think of any?"

Now Jude was looking into the dark backyard trying to come up with something. "You know, I think we need to be more disciplined about family vacations. It's getting harder and harder to schedule, and when we don't do it early and put it on the calendar, we end up defaulting to sports or other extracurricular stuff that isn't really very important in the grand scheme of things."

Theresa was nodding emphatically. "You know, we've been talking about that for the last three years, and somehow it always falls through the cracks."

"Of course it does. We've never had any context for it before."

"Write that down." Theresa commanded as she poured coffee.

"Write what down?"

"Context. I think that may be the key to all of this, giving a little context to the hundreds of things we need to do."

Jude was impressed by the insight, but teased his wife. "Wow. You really are much smarter than you look."

She threw a wadded-up paper towel at him. "Just write it down, wise guy."

He laughed and did as he was told.

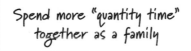

Spend more "quantity time" together as a family

Cut back on extracurricular activities	Cut back on social activities	Watch less television	Make family vacations a priority

"Anything else?" They both thought about it.

Theresa winced. "I hate to bring this up again, Jude."

He nodded. "I know, I know. You want me to cut back my travel."

She started to apologize as though she anticipated a protest. "It's just that I don't see how—"

He interrupted her. "No. You're right. I need to start being more discerning when it comes to getting on planes. I just have to do it."

Theresa was a little stunned. "Wow. Usually when I bring that up it turns into an argument."

"Like you said, it's all about context. Now that we have this goal of increasing family time, I realize that I have no choice. I know that sounds crazy, because it's not like I wanted to be away from home in the first place. But now it's crystal clear why I have to do it, and I honestly believe it will make a big difference."

He wrote down "Reduce Jude's travel" in yet another box.

```
┌─────────────────────────────────────────────┐
│        Spend more "quantity time"            │
│          together as a family                │
└─────────────────────────────────────────────┘
```

Cut back on extracurricular activities	Cut back on social activities	Watch less television	Make family vacations a priority	Reduce Jude's travel

They sat there looking at the boxes on the paper in front of Jude. Suddenly Theresa had an inspiration.

"You know, I think I should get off the school board."

Jude was surprised. "Well, first of all, that already falls under cutting back on extracurricular activities, so it's not another box. Second, I'm surprised you'd want to do that."

"Well, it's just that I think two years is enough. Right now it's more about me enjoying being on it and liking the fact that others know I'm on it. And I think that being a good mom is more important for the next few years. I can always be on the board when the kids are older."

Jude thought about her answer and nodded. "Makes sense to me."

Theresa was excited by the simplicity of what they'd just done. "This is really good. We've been complaining about and talking about making our lives less chaotic and more manageable for the last four years, but now we actually know what we need to do. If we can find ways to cut back on extracurriculars, do a little less socializing with other families, stop watching so much TV, make our family vacations a priority, and cut back on your travel a little, I can honestly say that it would make a big difference."

"You mean we wouldn't have to move to Appalachia?"

"I was thinking more like central Oregon. But no. We might not have to move."

"Oregon is nice," Jude put in, just to be ornery.

Theresa ignored his comment. "So, are we done here?" She wasn't so much tired as excited to get closure.

"Not quite. We have one last step. We've got to identify the regular, ongoing things we have to do to keep the family strong. We call them 'standard objectives' with our clients."

"I'm afraid you're going to have to explain that to me."

"Okay. Let's say I'm working with a widget manufacturer whose rallying cry is to increase its presence in the market by doing a new marketing campaign. The defining objectives might include redesigning the company logo, producing new television commercials, changing the Web site, hiring a new PR firm, that kind of stuff."

"Sounds good to me."

Jude continued. "But what happens if they do great on all those things, but let the rest of the business suffer? What about the stuff they have to do just to stay in business?"

"What kinds of things are you thinking about? Like sales?"

"Yeah. The stuff that is always important. Revenue, expenses, widget manufacturing, employee morale, customer satisfaction. Whatever was key to running their business last year and the year before that, as well as this year, next year, and the year after that."

Theresa was writing again. "So what would a family's standard objectives be?"

"You tell me." Now Jude was feeling like a professor.

Theresa stood to get more coffee. "Well, we have to keep an eye on our finances, just like a business."

Jude nodded and started yet another row of boxes beneath the others.

Theresa took a breath. "And we want to make sure we're doing everything for our health, like eating right and going to the doctor and exercising."

Jude wrote it down and nodded again, but this time more emphatically as if to say *you're on the right track, keep going*.

"Let me see. What else?" She came back to the table. "We need to make sure that our prayer life stays strong, of course. Church, Bible study, nightly prayers as a family."

He wrote it down. "Good. I think there are probably a few more."

Now Theresa closed her eyes and looked into her lap. "I think that education might be one of them. The kids need to be doing well in school and learning at the right pace." Before Jude could write that down, she had another one. "And I think we should put marriage on there too. We need to spend time together more regularly, going on dates, hanging out, playing kissy face."

Jude winced. "Gross."

She gently slapped him on the back of the head. "Just write it down."

He laughed and finished his chart by labeling each row.

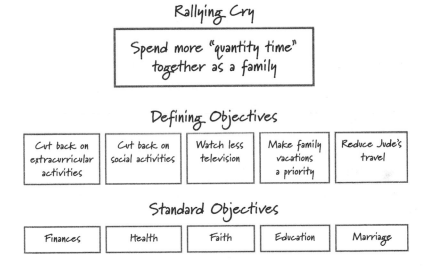

Rallying Cry

Spend more "quantity time" together as a family

Defining Objectives

Cut back on extracurricular activities	Cut back on social activities	Watch less television	Make family vacations a priority	Reduce Jude's travel

Standard Objectives

Finances	Health	Faith	Education	Marriage

Theresa took the paper now. "So the most important thing we have to do during the next six months or so is spend more time together as a family, without distractions or activities or external stress. Right?"

"I think that's a good way to say it."

Theresa went on. "And to do that, we have to focus on these five things." She pointed at the upper row of boxes.

Jude nodded. "That's right."

"And we can't forget to keep doing these things," she said, as she pointed at the lower row of boxes.

Jude smiled. "You got it."

Theresa stared at the page for a few seconds, and then smiled, shaking her head. "It just seems so simple."

"That's the whole idea. It should be simple. The point is not to have a plan with a thousand different to-do items. That's not what companies need, or families for that matter. They just need a clear overall priority to give them context, and then the basic building blocks of that priority."

Theresa was looking at the piece of paper as though it contained a secret formula for printing money. "I think this is really going to help."

"I do too."

Suddenly Theresa frowned. "But what do we do with it?"

"What do you mean?"

"I mean, how do we actually use it? And how do we avoid letting it collect dust in a folder somewhere?"

Jude was a little stunned by the question initially. Then something dawned on him.

"Oh, here's where families and companies differ. With my clients, we use this sheet of paper," he motioned at the one in Theresa's hands, "to run staff meetings. It is the basis for almost every conversation they have."

"Explain that to me."

"Well, at the beginning of every staff meeting, clients start by reviewing each of the boxes on the middle row, the defining objectives. How are we doing with the Web site, the TV commercials, the logo, the new PR firm? And then they look at the standard stuff in the lower row, like revenue, expenses, customer satisfaction, etcetera."

"Do they give themselves a grade? Are there some sort of metrics that they look at?"

Jude shook his head and smiled. "We have them use colors."

"Colors?"

"Yeah, colors. Red if something's bad. Yellow if it's going okay. Green if they're ahead of schedule or already finished."

Theresa was incredulous. "That's it?"

"Oh, no." Jude protested sarcastically. "We let them use orange and lime green too, for the times when they can't decide between two of the colors."

"Be serious, Jude."

"I am being serious. Our clients use the colors. And they like it."

"You're telling me that people running a business with reams of data and statistics go to staff meetings and rate their performance using green, yellow, and red?"

"They most certainly do. And they love it because it forces them to use their judgment to assess how they're doing. Don't get me wrong, though. They'll look at the numbers to confirm or deny what their guts are telling them. But they don't spend their time at meetings reviewing data. For one, that would be a waste of precious time. Second, it would be boring. And more important, the numbers aren't always telling the whole story. Sometimes the data's bad, and sometimes you might be measuring the wrong statistic."

"I still have a hard time believing that—"

Jude interrupted. "Okay, think about it in our family. Imagine we're reviewing our standard objective of keeping the kids educated. Do we have to pull out their report card or wait for the next round of grades to come out to assess how they're doing?"

He didn't let her answer. "Of course not. And we won't need a spreadsheet to tell us if I'm traveling less or if we're cutting back on extracurricular activities."

Theresa was buying into it all now, so Jude continued.

"Now, if I say that I think I've cut back my travel and you say that I haven't, we can certainly go to the calendar and add up the numbers to see what the truth is. But that's only if we have to. Executives are paid the big bucks for using their judgment in most cases. That's why very few CEOs are accountants. And I suppose that's why Ph.D.'s in psychology probably aren't necessarily the best parents either. It's about judgment and context more than expertise."

Theresa stood there, with a mix of confusion and amazement on her face. Gradually the confusion faded. "You know how you always say that what you do is not complicated?"

"Yeah."

"I always thought you were just being modest."

He smiled and responded in mock protest. "Are you saying I'm not modest?"

"No. Just that you were right."

"I'm not sure if that's a compliment or not."

She smiled and kissed him on the head. "Thanks for doing this."

"Can we go to bed now?"

"You can. I'm too excited."

"And full of caffeine."

"That too. But I really wish I could start testing this stuff and putting it into practice right now."

Her opportunity would come sooner than she could have imagined, and it would prove a little painful.

THE INCIDENT

wo days later, Theresa was sitting in carpool, her minivan one of a long line of utility vehicles waiting to gobble up uniformed children spilling out of cinderblock classrooms. Her phone rang, and she looked to see who it was. The caller I.D. said "Kelly Horan." Before she could answer it, she heard a horn honk behind her and looked in her rearview mirror and saw the Horan family minivan.

Theresa clicked on her cell phone. "You're a bad girl, Mrs. Horan. You know we're not supposed to talk on our cell phones in carpool."

"I know. I've always been a rebel. I just called to tell you that you'll be glad to know that there are three empty coffee cups on the floor of my van right now. And that I haven't even showered today."

Theresa laughed. "How did you know that would make me happy?"

"Oh, I had a feeling."

And then it happened. Theresa released just enough pressure from the brake under her right foot to allow her van to roll forward until it made contact with the Suburban in front of her.

"Oh, crap! I just hit the car in front of me. Gotta go." She hung up, checked on Michael, and waited to see what the other driver, most likely another mom, would do. After what seemed like a minute, the door opened and out stepped a youngish, tiny woman who seemed to have trouble climbing down from her perch in the driver's seat.

Fortunately for Theresa, she didn't seem angry or overly concerned. In fact, she was smiling as though she were anticipating the embarrassment of the driver behind her.

Theresa stepped out of her minivan. "I am so sorry."

Before she even saw if there was damage, the petite woman smiled. "Oh, you barely touched me. I'm sure it's fine." They arrived at the point of contact at the same time and were both relieved that there was no visible evidence of the micro collision. Two minutes later, both women were back in their cars.

As unremarkable as the fender bump had been, it generated some attention from the largely unoccupied moms sitting in their vehicles nearby. Worse yet, it caught the attention of the carpool attendant for the day, which happened to be the school's principal.

Now, Theresa knew Mrs. Hourigan well and wasn't expecting a tongue-lashing from her. But as sweet as the principal was, she did have a well-deserved reputation as a stickler for details and rules. So Theresa put her cell phone in her purse in the hopes of concealing any evidence of her crime.

"Everything okay, Mrs. Cousins?" Mrs. Hourigan knew the first names of most of the parents in her school, but liked to refer to them more formally when students were around. "It doesn't look like there's even a scratch."

"Yeah, lucky for me." Suddenly she felt a need to confess and seemed to have lost control of what she was saying. "Stupid me, I was talking on my cell phone."

Mrs. Hourigan gave Theresa a mock scowl. "Shame on you. I might have to keep you in detention."

They laughed.

"Actually, there is something I wanted to ask you about."

Theresa, feeling a little vulnerable, was glad to have the subject changed. "What is it?"

"Well, as you know, next week is the school auction."

"Yep. Jude and I will be there."

"Great." She paused. "Well, I'd like to line up our chairpersons for next year's auction so we can announce it then. I think you and Jude would be great, and I'm really hoping you'll do it."

Like a deer in the headlights, Theresa froze. But somehow, her mouth didn't. After the cell phone infraction, she felt compelled to please Mrs. Hourigan. "We would be honored." It was as though her life were passing before her eyes. *Did I just say that?*

And before she could put the words back in her mouth, Mrs. Hourigan was hugging her through the window. "Oh, I am so excited. I just know that you'll do a great job. Do you know how happy I am and how glad I am that I saw you today?"

Theresa smiled and feigned excitement. Inside, she was screaming *noooooo!!!*

SECOND CONFESSION

Theresa broke the news to Jude that night over dinner. She decided that having the kids around might diminish the magnitude of his reaction.

After telling him about the happenings of the day and the seemingly inconsequential fender bender in the school parking lot, she went for it.

"And then I did something horrific and terrible and ridiculous. And you're not going to like it."

Jude was a little stunned, but he smiled. "I'm sure it's not that bad. What is it?"

"In a moment of weakness, I told Mrs. Hourigan that we'd be in charge of the auction next year."

Jude didn't immediately digest the magnitude of what his wife had just told him. Perhaps her frightening intro had lulled him into a temporary state of relief. In a matter of seconds, however, he came to.

"Why in the world would you do that?"

Theresa explained how the embarrassment of the situation had caught her off guard and made her vulnerable.

Jude took a breath. "Okay, let's not panic here. Just call her tomorrow and tell her you made a mistake."

Theresa nodded, but wasn't on board yet. "But what do I say? What's my excuse? Jude, you should have seen how happy she was."

"Is her happiness going to make you feel better when you're running around the Bay Area all summer asking every restaurant and jeweler and hotel and department store for donations? I can't believe you did this."

And that's when something dawned on Theresa.

MOMENT OF TRUTH

"I'll be right back," Theresa said. And without another word she left the room. Jude started collecting dishes and scooping out ice cream for the girls, and even a little for Michael. Before he had set the last of the desserts down, Theresa returned, looking decidedly more peaceful than she had just ten minutes ago.

Noticing the change, Jude had to ask. "Where did you go?"

"To make a phone call."

"Who did you call?"

"Mrs. Hourigan. I told her that my biggest priority this year was to spend more time at home with my family, and that as much as I'd like to help her, and as much as I'd like her to think of me as willing to do whatever she asked, it wouldn't be right for the family."

Jude was a little stunned. "Whoa. What did she say?"

"She congratulated me for having my priorities in order, and she asked me if I knew of anyone who might have the time and the talent to do a good job. In fact, she put me in charge of helping her recruit someone, which I gladly agreed to do."

Jude smiled proudly at his wife. "I guess the rallying cry works."

Theresa nodded. "Maybe it does."

FINISHING

With a little more confidence—and a few nights of sleep—Theresa decided it was time to finalize the Cousins Family Plan. Luckily, Molly from next door was available and in need of spending money, so Theresa brought her over to watch the kids so she'd be able to focus. She then went into her bedroom and sprawled out on the floor.

Just twenty-five minutes later, to Theresa's amazement, she was done. When Jude came home from work, she handed it to him for his review before saying hello. He was surprised by the brevity of the document, as well as its clarity.

When Jude came into the kitchen after reading the short document, he had hoped to make some sort of joke. But he couldn't keep the smile off his face. "This is terrific."

"You think so?"

"Come on. You know it's terrific. I can't wait to go get a whiteboard and get all this stuff down. You did a great job, Theresa. Really."

What makes the Cousins family unique?

We're a large, close family where the parents are immersed in the lives of their children. The family's life is centered around church and faith, and we believe in being passionate and emotionally invested in everything we do.

What is the most important priority in our lives right now?

Between now and Christmas, the Cousins family will take steps to spend more peaceful, alone time together as a family.

To do that we will:

- Make difficult decisions about eliminating extracurricular activities.
- Cut back slightly on our social calendar.
- Reduce Jude's travel.
- Cut back on television for everyone in the family.
- Be more proactive about planning vacations.

We will also have to stay on top of our regular responsibilities:

- Maintain a vibrant faith life.
- Work to stay healthy.
- Be responsible about our finances.
- Help the children become well educated.
- Keep our marriage strong.

How will we keep these things alive?

- We will have ten-minute meetings once a week to assess how well we're doing.
- We will put all of this material on a whiteboard in the kitchen so that we are constantly reminded of how we will make decisions in a consistent way.
- We will revisit our rallying cry in three months and decide if it is time for a new one.

Not comfortable with compliments, Theresa shifted her focus to the matter at hand. "Can you imagine if we actually hold ourselves accountable for doing this? It will be a different world."

Jude nodded. "But don't get too far ahead of yourself. There's still going to be craziness."

"I know, I know. But at least we're not going to feel quite so," she hesitated, "*victimized* by it all. I just want to have a say in the craziness."

He nodded. "So, can I go to Staples right now and get the whiteboard?"

"No. It's dinner time." She smiled. "Besides, I want to get it."

RETRAINING

Theresa decided that it wouldn't be fair, or wise, to try to bring her guinea pig friends back together for another lesson. Instead, she would take it upon herself to teach them and their husbands, one by one. She started with the family she thought would be easiest: Rob and Linda Groninger. Fortunately, she proved right.

Sitting down at the Groninger kitchen table one evening while their girls were doing homework in another part of the house, Theresa began by admitting that she was a little nervous because Rob knew the fundamentals behind her theories better than she did.

But he set her straight. "Listen, Theresa. Our family is as scattered as the next, and I'm obviously not using any of this stuff at home. So don't assume that you're preaching to the choir here. And besides, you need to be able to do this with confidence and conviction."

Linda was a little stunned at the directness of her husband's command. But it turned out to be exactly what Theresa needed to hear.

"Okay, here's the thing. What our families lack more than anything else is context. We're waking up every day and winging it, without much to guide us or give us perspective. And that's what we're going to change tonight."

Linda sat upright. "Well, don't you sound authoritative."

Theresa laughed. "Isn't that what you wanted?" she asked Rob.

"Absolutely. Keep going."

She then explained the three questions, and directed most of her lecture at Linda. To Theresa's relief and joy, Rob seemed as interested as his wife.

One by one, Theresa explained the meaning behind the questions. She talked about a family's core values, and because she knew the family well, helped the Groningers quickly identify three or four candidates. Then she took them through the strategy exercise, something that Rob was particularly impressed with.

"Did your husband help you with this assignment?" he teased.

Theresa pretended to be incredulous. "Are you kidding? I haven't talked to him about this once. This is all me, baby."

They laughed.

"Well, whatever the case, you've nailed the strategy part."

For the next fifteen minutes they debated what the foundations of the Groninger family strategy might be. Whenever they got bogged down, Theresa would say,

"Don't worry about making it perfect. Just get it going in the right direction."

Finally, the Groningers settled on two, and wrote their rough draft of a paragraph to answer question one.

We are a family that values candor and humor and forgiveness. Our extended family is our primary set of friends. And we're committed to public service and volunteerism.

Linda had a question. "Now, I'm still a little confused. Is the public service part a value or a strategy?"

"Don't worry about it. It doesn't matter. It's all mixed together. What matters is that it's part of who you are."

Linda gladly heeded her friend's advice.

Theresa pushed on to the second question. "So, what is the top priority for the Groninger family right now?"

"You mean this week, this month, or this year?" Linda wanted to know.

"How about over the course of the next two to six months?" She paused and looked at Rob. "Remind me why that's the usual time frame?"

"Well, in our practice, it all depends on the nature of the client and what's happening. A small company in a crisis will have a very short-term rallying cry. A government agency or a university will almost always have a longer one. The key is, if it's shorter than a couple months, you won't have enough time to make progress. If it's longer than a year, it's too far out there to start thinking about. Somewhere in between is usually right, and I think for a family two to six months sounds about right."

"Let's make ours two months," Linda suggested. "I'm too impatient to think beyond that."

Theresa steered her a little. "That's fine, but let's see what the goal is first. I'm guessing that will help us figure out how long it should take."

Rob nodded his agreement, and they began. In just five minutes, Linda suggested a rallying cry.

"Remodel the house."

Silence.

Sensing their disapproval, "What's wrong with that?"

Rob went first. "Well, I realize that we're going to be remodeling. But we certainly aren't going to be done in two to six months. We don't have a final architectural plan. We haven't figured out the financing completely."

Linda looked at Theresa. "That means we've been arguing about it a lot."

Rob smiled and went on. "And the approvals alone will take weeks or months. So I think the rallying cry should be something shorter, maybe one of the first big steps in the process."

They thought about it for a moment.

"Are you guys sure that's the most important thing going on right now?"

The husband and wife looked at each other, and responded almost in unison. "Oh, yeah."

Rob explained. "It's causing us stress almost every day. We can't figure out if we want to do a complete teardown, or remodel a little at a time. There are financial factors. Will we have to move out? What can we really afford?"

Linda spoke next. "So how about if the rallying cry is just a two-month goal, and it's to finalize all the plans for the remodel? The other kind of goals—what do you call them?"

"Defining objectives," Theresa answered.

"The defining objectives would be to decide on what we want, get the drawings done, choose a contractor, and finalize financing. Once we get that done, we can move on to the next phase."

Theresa and Rob looked at one another as if to say, *sounds good.* Theresa then wrote "finalize plans for remodel" in a large box at the top of the page, and the defining objectives that Linda had just identified in boxes below it.

She then took the Groningers through the quick process of identifying their standard objectives, which turned out to be very similar to those of the Cousins.

Finances, Family (extended), Faith, Fidelity (marriage), and Feducation.

Rob really wanted to make them all start with the same letter.

Finally, Theresa asked question number three. "So, how are you going to use this? How often are you going to talk about your progress?"

Linda was confident. "Well, if we don't do it at least once a week, it's going to disappear."

They agreed on having a weekly meeting for ten minutes every Sunday night, as well as making a small poster of what they had just done that would be put on the refrigerator.

And just like that, less than ninety minutes after arriving, Theresa was walking out the door with her first counseling session done.

Sadly, her next one would not be so easy.

TOUGH LOVE

Theresa decided that Alison and Scott Marsh would be her next test case. She and Jude had known them for a number of years, and had even vacationed with them once in Oregon. Scott and Jude golfed occasionally, and were certainly friends, if not close ones.

Theresa thought that their closeness would make Scott more open to her ideas than a less familiar husband. As it turned out, however, Scott's familiarity with Theresa only made him feel more comfortable dismissing her. And being a little inconsiderate, too.

"Can I stay in the den and watch the ball game and have you guys tell me what you come up with when you're done?" he asked earnestly.

Alison's reaction had a tinge of humor in it. "Don't be such a doofus, Scott. This isn't my family. It's ours. You can sit here for the next . . . ." She stopped and looked at Theresa. "How long is this going to take?"

"Forty-five minutes, maybe an hour."

Alison picked up where she'd left off. "You can sit here for the next hour. Besides, you can TiVo the baseball game and watch it later tonight."

Less than excited by his wife's entreaty, Scott came to the kitchen table and sat down.

Concerned about holding his attention, Theresa went fast. "Okay, this is all about giving the Marsh family a little more context so that you can make decisions and live your lives in a more purposeful, less frantic manner."

Scott winced. "I'm sorry, Theresa. I don't mean to be difficult right out of the gate here, but I don't know that I'd describe our family as being frantic. Sure, it's a little busy at times, but I wouldn't say *frantic*."

Theresa didn't know what to say. Alison did.

"Excuse me? What family are you part of, Scott? We are totally frantic. Do you remember last weekend?"

Scott wasn't ready to relent. "I don't know. Maybe it's because I've been working more lately, and you've been doing most of the home stuff. But it doesn't seem so bad to me."

Alison calmed down a bit. "Yeah, maybe it's because you haven't been around as much lately. But I think that's part of our problem."

Now Scott got just a little defensive. "It's not like I'm gone all the time. I don't think things have changed that much since I started working more."

"Are you kidding? Do you really believe that, Scott?'

He shrugged. "I just don't think it's been that bad."

Alison winced. "Well, I don't want to get too personal here in front of Theresa—"

Scott interrupted. "I'm sure she can handle it." He had no clue what his wife was about to say.

Alison hesitated, took a breath, and smiled. "Okay, then. Does it strike you as odd that we haven't been," she paused as if she were searching for the right word, "intimate with each other much for the past six months?"

Scott's eyebrows shot up. "Whoa. Maybe she didn't need to hear that."

They all laughed.

"Nothing I haven't heard before," Theresa assured them.

Alison continued. "Scott, we're not anywhere near as cohesive as we ought to be. And it's not getting better. It's getting worse. And you're right. I'm feeling it more than you, especially now that I'm working too."

Scott wasn't ready to give in. "Listen, we bought that new computer, and you have a BlackBerry now. If you can't get organized with all of that, then—"

Now Theresa interrupted. "I don't think *organized* is the right word, Scott. It's more about being clear about who you are and what's important. Like you do at work."

Scott rolled his eyes. "My work is a bad example. Our practice is completely screwed up. The managing doc doesn't have a clue. We are flailing so bad it's not even funny."

Theresa wanted to kick herself for not remembering Alison's comment about Scott's job being tumultuous. She regrouped. "What do you mean by flailing?"

Recounting the dysfunction at work made Scott a little more emotional now. "I don't know. We're always reacting to whatever the other orthopedic doctors in the area do. We wait for a patient to complain before coming up with a plan. And then everything is suddenly a top priority and everyone's scrambling around trying to implement some new and ridiculous initiative. And two weeks later, there's some other new initiative. I barely have enough time to see my regular patients, let alone get more of them. It's a circus."

Knowing that his frustration wasn't meant for her, Theresa pushed back. "So, there's no clarity then?"

Still agitated. "Clarity? Are you kidding? Those idiots couldn't describe what they're trying to do if they wanted to."

Alison now put her hand on Scott's shoulder, just to calm him a bit. It worked.

He took a breath. "I'm sorry, you guys. It's just so crazy right now, and I don't seem to have any control or influence. I'm working longer hours than ever, have nothing to show for it, and if things continue like this I'm going to be out of a job."

Theresa didn't hesitate before she responded. "It sounds like that would be a good thing."

The room froze as though she had just told Scott to jump off a bridge.

Rather than sit in the awkwardness of the moment, Theresa kept talking. "I mean, why would you want to work there if it's so awful? And don't get me wrong, it does sound awful."

Alison chimed in, gently. "We did talk about this a few years ago, Scott. About you getting out of there and going out on your own. Or finding a smaller, less political practice closer to home."

Scott shook his head. "Listen, I'm a doctor, not an accountant. When you join a big practice you just don't think about hopping from one place to another. And the thought of opening up my own office is just too. . . . " He hesitated and didn't look like he was going to finish the sentence.

"Too what?" Theresa asked.

"I don't know. I don't think I'd be able to set it up and deal with all the administration."

"Why not?" Alison was incredulous. "You graduated at the top of your friggin medical school class. Why in the world would you not be able to open your own orthopedic practice? Heck, I could help you. It'd be fun."

Scott sat there looking at his wife as though a good excuse were printed somewhere on her face. After two full and pronounced breaths, he finally spoke. "Really?"

"Absolutely. I could find you an office near Valley hospital in no time flat. You'd have no problem getting referrals from there. And your sister-in-law is an insurance broker, you meathead, so she could handle all that."

Scott actually seemed open to the idea, if not a little excited. "Well, you're the entrepreneur in the family. But let's not get ahead of ourselves here."

Now Alison was getting excited. "You know something, Theresa? I think this is our biggest challenge as a family."

"What?"

"Scott."

Scott raised his eyebrows. "Excuse me?"

Alison explained. "I think that until we get your work situation in a better place, we're not going to be in any position to make progress. From the hours you're working to the commute to your depr—" she caught herself, "your frustration, even the intimacy stuff. It's all tied up in your work."

After taking it all in, Scott decided to correct his wife. "Wait a second. If I'm being honest, it's more than just my work. I'm in worse physical shape than I've ever been. I'm grumpy to the kids, and that's not my nature. I'm not enjoying much of anything these days." He looked at Theresa. "I haven't golfed with Jude in a year and a half. And Alison and I haven't gone on a real date since Valentine's Day, more than six months ago."

Alison was glad to hear his candor. "I think you're right. We need to get you to a good place. That's the biggest thing our family needs to do."

Scott frowned. "But this shouldn't be just about me. That makes me seem like I'm the most important person in the family. I don't like that."

Alison teased him. "Don't worry, honey. You're not the most important person in the family. Charlie is." Charlie was their youngest son. "But right now, helping you get back on track is more important than anything else."

He winced, still uncomfortable.

"Think about it this way." Now Theresa was going to take a shot at convincing him. "You can't help the family in the way you need to if you're not strong. And based on what you've been saying, you don't seem too strong right now."

Scott shook his head. "I'm definitely not strong."

Theresa was strangely energized. "Okay. Now we're getting somewhere."

For the next forty-five minutes, the group of friends went back through the first question, about values and strategy, and then talked about how they would go about using it.

Scott, now a convert to whatever it was that Theresa was peddling, couldn't stop asking questions. Alison had to force him to move forward on a number of occasions, knowing that he would have kept Theresa there until midnight if he had his way.

By nine o'clock, the Marshes had a plan and Theresa went home confident that her system actually worked.

What makes the Marsh family unique?

The Marsh family likes competition, humor, and hard work. The anchors for how they live their lives are a focus on learning, spending time at their vacation home in Lake Tahoe, and spending much of their social lives with local aunts, uncles, and cousins.

What is the most important priority in our lives right now?

In the next two months, the Marsh family will work to get Scott healthy.

To do that we will:
- Exercise regularly
- Vent about job when helpful
- Go on regular dates with Alison
- Explore career options: Join new practice or start own
- Consider counseling

We will also have to stay on top of our regular responsibilities:
- Financial strength
- Physical health
- Spiritual health/prayer
- Marriage/family
- Fun

How will we keep these things alive?
- Weekly review of goals during dates
- Whiteboard in family room with goals, values, and strategy

ROLLING ON

Over the next two weeks, Theresa diligently revisited each of the friends that had come to her house for lunch that day, and she discovered two things. First, her approach worked in virtually every family, regardless of the circumstance. Second, every family's plan was different, some wildly so.

One family would have an extremely tactical rallying cry, while another would have a life-changing one. One family's values or strategy would seem novel while the next would be relatively standard. But as Theresa always explained, regardless of their different levels of novelty, all that mattered was that the answers were honest and true.

Though Theresa was disappointed that one of her friends gave up on her clarity plan, deciding that chaos was inevitable and that having a meeting every week was just too much work, her confidence in the system wasn't shaken by the single failure. And deep down inside she hoped—and even expected—that the woman would be calling Theresa back one day when she was ready to make another run at sanity. Besides, that failure was more than offset by two unexpected success stories.

When Alison Marsh's sister, who was recently married but didn't have children, heard about the three big questions, she was able to apply them to her own family life, with great success. "Listen, my husband and I may not have kids, but somehow life finds a way to be chaotic for us, too. This gives us a sense of clarity and is helping us think through decisions about our future."

One of Jude's first clients and a friend of the Cousins family, Kathryn Petersen, had an even more surprising story. She and her husband had recently retired and were struggling with their newly found freedom—and occasional boredom. After learning about Theresa's project, they created new goals for themselves, which Kathryn explained in a thank-you e-mail sent to Theresa. "As a result of your system, we're starting a nonprofit, and we're moving closer to our children and grandchildren. I'm not sure we would ever have had that conversation without having to answer the three big questions."

As elated as she was by the unexpected applications, Theresa found that her confidence in her approach was boosted most by her own experience. By Christmas Eve, her fortieth birthday and Michael's second, Theresa and Jude had made remarkable strides toward increasing and enhancing the time the Cousins family spent at home. That progress was a result of nothing more than finally focusing on what mattered most to them.

The evidence was clear. With just a little prompting from their mom and dad, the twins agreed that swimming would become a recreational activity instead of a competitive one, which meant no more swim practices and meets during half the year. Jude decided that he could afford to limit his consulting practice to West Coast clients, making overnight trips both rarer and shorter. And of course, Theresa stepped down from her position on the school board, overcoming the good-natured pleading of Principal Hourigan.

Beyond eliminating activities, Theresa and Jude added a few. Thursday night dates—without friends or children—became an almost inviolable ritual in the Cousins schedule, with Friday nights set aside for the whole family, which usually meant board games or movies. And the annual summer vacation was now booked before Christmas, so that work and sports events could be scheduled around it. There was no doubt that the Cousins family was in a more confident, less frantic state than it had been since, well, since its inception.

But none of the evidence would prepare Theresa for the call she would receive a few weeks later. It was from Candace Barrington.

"I have a big favor to ask of you." Candace sounded hesitant. "Carrie has suddenly decided that she doesn't want to play on a traveling soccer team this year. I don't know what's gotten into her, but she told me that if she has to train three nights a week ten months of the year, she'd rather not play at all."

Theresa fought the urge to even think the words *I told you so.*

"Anyway, if there is any way that she could play on Jude's team . . ." She didn't finish the sentence.

After a brief pause to make sure that Candace was done talking, Theresa jumped in and assured her that Jude would call her back and do everything he could to help Carrie. And when she hung up the phone, she looked at the white-board hanging on the wall in the kitchen and thought to herself, *how did we survive without context?*

FAST-FORWARD

As the new year began, Theresa and Jude decided it was time for a new rallying cry. To their surprise, it took just ten minutes to come up with one. The focus of the family's collective efforts for the next four months would become Michael, their two-year-old, who had been slightly overlooked during much of his young life, and especially during the recent scramble to get the rest of the Cousins household in order.

As a result of his attention deficit, he was a little behind where his sisters had been at his age in most observable categories, including talking, sleeping, and discipline. Some of this was certainly due to the coddling of his parents, who treated the baby of the family like, well, a baby. But it was time, Theresa and Jude decided, to put him back on track.

To make that happen, Theresa and Jude would have to put him on a consistent sleep regimen, which would include resisting the temptation to bring him into bed with them at night. It would also require a few sessions with a language therapist and the more rigorous use of time-out sessions.

Michael's sisters would pitch in by doing more frequent baby-sitting, both to help their mother and to give their brother the sisterly attention that had been too scarce during the last two years of hyperactivity and overscheduling.

Even though their rallying cry had changed, the Cousins family's standard objectives would remain the same, as would their values and strategy. In fact, those wouldn't need to change at all for the next few years, providing a sense of stability and consistency amid the regular resetting of priorities.

Over that time an oversized whiteboard would become something of an unattractive but beloved fixture in the Cousins kitchen. Across the top of the wood-framed board Theresa wrote the description of what made her family unique. In the body of the board, she wrote her thematic goal in a single box toward the top. Below that she wrote the five defining objectives in a line of horizontal boxes, and beneath that, another row of boxes depicting the family's standard objectives. Above each box, she put a circle that she would fill in with colors to indicate the "score" for each category.

That cluttered board would become an inevitable topic of conversation for any new visitors, and would be duplicated with minor modifications in more and more homes throughout the area.

Cousins Family Scoreboard

Our Rallying Cry

We're a large, close family where the parents are immersed in the lives of their children. Our life is centered around church and faith, and we believe in being passionate and emotionally invested in everything we do.

Refocus on Michael's development

Defining Objectives

Implement consistent sleep schedule	Address language capabilities and deficiencies	Introduce time-out sessions	Establish extra reading time	Involve sisters more in play and work

Standard Objectives

Finances	Health	Faith	Education	Marriage

● Green ● Yellow ● Red

Over time, enough people heard about Theresa's system that she began doing annual workshops at St. Anthony's and other schools in the area. Whenever he could, Jude would go to those sessions and watch from the back of the room.

On one evening, toward the end of her presentation, a young dad wearing a suit raised his hand to ask a question. Or so Theresa thought.

When she called on him, the man stood up, cleared his throat, and announced with a mixture of frustration and delight, "You know, if the executives at work ran our company the way you do your family, we wouldn't be on the verge of going out of business."

Startled, Theresa spotted Jude in the back of the room and flashed him an expression of surprise and excitement. All he could do was smile.

The Model

THE FRANTIC FAMILY

The vast majority of families I know—including my own—would admit that one or more of the following adjectives apply to them: *reactive, scattered, frantic, chaotic, stressed.*

And if you were to ask them if they were living their lives with the sense of purpose and intentionality that they want, every last one of them would look at you like you were mocking them and say, "Are you kidding?"

At first glance, this is almost humorous. Complaining about the crazy lives we lead is something of a rite of passage in our culture. Unfortunately, society is facing a serious epidemic of chaos in families, the cost of which is both real and painful.

In addition to general increases in levels of disappointment and stress, rates of depression, substance abuse, and psychological disorder are rising drastically. And this is especially true among middle- and upper-class families who are overwhelmed by the unfocused day-to-day lives they lead.

Kids who are being shuttled from school to soccer to ballet to baseball to piano lessons to birthday parties to counselors to tutors to athletic trainers are not turning out the way their parents want. And parents who are doing all of that shuttling and working and cooking and cleaning and socializing and exercising are not feeling fulfilled. They are looking at one another and wondering, "Is this inevitable? Is this how it's supposed to be?" And when they see everyone else scattered and stressed like they are, they're coming to the conclusion that maybe it is.

I'm here to say that it is not supposed to be this way, and it is certainly not inevitable. Yes, life should be busy and demanding at times, but it should also be lived with a sense of purpose and sanity that allows us to be the people we're meant to be. And I don't think anyone is meant to be perpetually tired and stressed.

What is it that our families are lacking that causes all of this? Do we need more discipline? More structure? Perhaps, but those are not the main culprits here, and improvements in those areas alone will not reduce the craziness we feel at home. Not without something else that is as simple as it is critical. I'm talking about context.

CONTEXT

ontext is one of those words that gets used a lot but is hard to define without using the word itself. I went to dictionary.com and found this definition:

Context (kon-tekst): the set of circumstances or facts that surround a particular event, situation, etc.

When it comes to families, I might define it in a slightly different way. Context is the information and framework we need to make a decision in the most informed, intentional manner possible.

Without context, every decision that confronts us, every situation we encounter, calls for unnecessary anxiety, stressful uncertainty, and unproductive conflict. Which, in turn, makes our lives much more challenging than they need to be.

This is all a shame because running a family, though difficult, should not be complicated. Like most things in life—marriage, parenting, leadership, physical fitness, financial stability—it comes down to mastering a handful of simple concepts, which requires more persistence and dedication than it does intelligence.

In fact, most of us already know what it takes to make our families more effective and sane; we just have this tendency, when faced with a little stress, to forget. As the eighteenth-century author Samuel Johnson once said, "People need to be reminded more often than they need to be instructed."

What is it that we need to be reminded about? Yes, context.

None of us would think about running a business without it. Even the leaders of most mediocre companies sit down and try to figure out what their priorities are, how they differ from their competition, and what their unique advantages or disadvantages might be. They don't just wing it, even if it sometimes looks that way to an outsider.

And in our personal lives we understand the need for context in many of the decisions we make. We don't buy a car or book a vacation without asking ourselves a series of questions that will give us a framework for making a good decision. We'll often jot down a list of important criteria. How many people will I be driving? How much money do I want to spend? Would I rather vacation in a hot or cold climate? Do I want to fly or drive to get there? Simple stuff that we instinctively recognize as being necessary in order to be purposeful—and successful—in whatever we're doing.

And yet most of us go about leading and managing our families with almost no formal context. We don't take time to explicitly decide who we are, what we stand for, what we want, and how we're going to go about succeeding and thriving as a family. Why don't we?

Because we don't think of our families as the organizations they are, in need of leadership and planning and strategy. We also feel a little awkward or embarrassed by taking a somewhat formal approach to managing our families, deciding that it sounds silly or overly structured. Finally, we somehow fail to see the cost of our chaos, and the connection it has to real problems like poor mental and physical health, financial failure, and even divorce.

And so we go on living context-free lives, taking on every decision and issue in a relatively isolated way, as though it weren't part of a larger situation. And then we wonder why each day feels like a disconnected, reactive game of survival, a grind without the kind of purposeful progress that we all crave.

Until that changes, until we achieve some simple clarity around the context of our families, no amount of discipline or structure is going to amount to much.

Now if I were reading this book, right about now I would be asking the question, "How long is it going to take to create this context, and how soon before I see any results?" That leads us to the next section.

FAST, FAST, FAST

Providing context and reducing chaos in our families can—and should—happen very quickly. That's because the solution I am suggesting here was developed with two of my favorite aphorisms in mind.

THE 80/20 RULE (ALSO KNOWN AS THE PARETO PRINCIPLE)

Basically, this rule promotes the idea that 80 percent of the value of any endeavor comes from the first 20 percent of the work. Beyond that, diminishing marginal returns set in. And when it comes to helping you get context in your family, I believe that the first hour or so of the work will provide most of the benefits. That's right, implementing the suggestions that follow should take no more than sixty minutes up front and ten minutes a week. More important, it will be liberating and even fun. Really.

DON'T MAKE THE PERFECT
THE ENEMY OF THE GOOD

This second adage is somewhat similar to the first because
it calls for us to embrace the fact that a good, simple plan
that can be implemented quickly is better than a perfect
one that takes months and years to put into practice (and
that usually amounts to nothing when you throw up your
hands and quit!). Or as I like to say to my wife when she's
undertaking a project and gets bogged down in making it
perfect, "if something's worth doing, it's worth doing half-
assed." That's not exactly the way we were taught as kids,
but when it comes to making our family lives less scattered
and harried, perfection is just not an option.

* * * *

Why am I confident that this can work?

It's not because I'm a family expert with years of experience and research under my belt. I'm just a management consultant who helps CEOs and other leaders build
healthier organizations with greater context and clarity. I'm
also a husband and parent of four children, and our family
is as frantic and chaotic and reactive as the next one, if not
a little more so.

One day it dawned on me that the principles I write
about and speak about and teach to my clients could work
in my family. About that same time I started noticing that
more and more people were approaching me after my talks

to say, "You know, I would think this stuff would work at home, too."

So I tweaked some of my consulting principles and geared them for home life. When I explained them to clients and other moms and dads I met, their reaction was usually along these lines: "You have to write a book about that!" or "Hurry up and write that book!" or "Can you send me your manuscript so I can go over it with my husband this weekend?"

And that's basically how this book came about. By accident. Out of desperation. Through trial and error. But as the saying goes, sometimes necessity is the mother of invention.

THE THREE
BIG QUESTIONS

Okay then, in order to restore sanity and clarity to our families, we must answer and act upon three big, simple questions.

1. *What makes your family unique?* If you don't know what differentiates your family from others, you won't have a basis for making decisions, and you'll try to be all things to all people.

2. *What is your family's top priority—rallying cry—right now?* You need to know what the single most important objective is for your family over the next two to six months. Without a top priority, everything becomes important and you end up reacting to whatever issues seem urgent that day.

3. *How do you talk about and use the answers to these questions?* If you answer the first two questions but don't use those answers in daily, weekly, and monthly decision-making, it will yield no benefits.

Let's explore these simple but critical questions one at a time.

QUESTION #1

What makes your family unique?

Another way to phrase this question is, what differentiates your family from every other one on your block, or at your school, or in your church? Two primary topics help us identify our uniqueness: values and strategy. I'll explain each of them separately, but want to stress up front that identifying them need not be an overly rigid, complex, or disciplined process. In fact, sometimes just answering the simple question "what makes us unique?" will get you there.

CORE VALUES

These are the fundamental and positive qualities that are undeniable about your family, something that would be almost impossible to suppress even if you wanted to do so. Identifying your family's core values should be neither time-consuming nor difficult. In fact, it is usually an interesting and enjoyable discussion for parents to have. The key to identifying your core values is realizing that you should have just two or three, and that all the good qualities under the sun—as wonderful and desirable as they might be—are not necessarily good candidates to be called core for your family.

A good way to start searching for core values is for parents to think about what inspired their relationship in the first place, and what it was about one another that made them consider getting married. Here's how it worked in one particular family that served as a loose model for the Cousins family in the story.

When the husband first met his wife in college, he always admired how she would call out the truth, even when it wasn't socially or politically correct. If something was wrong, she would say, "I'm sorry, I just don't think that's right." She wasn't rude or difficult, but she wasn't afraid to be the lone dissenter either. Now, that may sound small, but when he was in college it was rare. More important, it was something he admired about her and still does today.

As it turned out, his wife saw the same quality in him, and after dating for a while, they came to realize that it was a commonly held value. Today, after going through this exercise, they've begun to talk to their kids more purposefully about the importance of standing up for what is right, even when it isn't popular. Also, they won't make a decision for their family that would contradict that value.

Another value they've identified is what they call *passion for whatever you're doing*. Essentially, they believe in choosing activities and jobs and hobbies that they're excited about and that provide a level of personal fulfillment. They've been involved in everything from writing travel books and songs to inventing a board game to acting and putting together a musical. They don't come from families that were involved in—or for that matter, really encouraged—those things. It's just who they are, and it's part of what makes their family unique.

One way to know if you've identified a core value is to ask yourself if you occasionally take it a little too far. For instance, if this particular family really believes that standing up for what is right is at their core, then they're probably going to be a little more strident about a perceived injustice than they need to be at times. And that's okay, because if a value is truly core, you'll accept the occasional and inevitable exaggeration of it, even if there is a cost.

Consider that their value around passion sometimes leads them to launch into creative projects that are beyond their ability to follow through. Some of their friends and extended family members tease them for being impractical dreamers. And they'll gladly—or maybe not so gladly—tolerate those labels because they speak to what makes them who they are.

And since they're raising their kids with their core values in mind, they can't be shocked if the kids too might take those values to extremes at times. In fact, they've discovered that their daughters sometimes get a little more indignant than they should about something they think is unfair. Though they will certainly teach the girls to exercise good judgment in assessing how to respond to those situations effectively and appropriately, they can't do so in a way that punishes them and confuses them about what they stand for as a family.

Now, one of the problems that families—and companies, for that matter—have with values is that they end up with too many. To avoid this, families must have the courage to differentiate between values that are core, and others that are not. For instance, some values are desirable but not true. We call these "aspirational values" because they are worthy of our aspirations. Other types of values that can get confused with core are what we call "permission-to-play values." These are universally desirable traits like honesty, integrity, and fairness. As important as they are, they have become almost generic and represent a minimum standard of behavior.

When families confuse aspirational and permission-to-play values with core, they end up adopting a long list of every positive adjective in the world. Not only does this make them sound generically delusional, it fails to differentiate them from every other family that wants to be perfect, including the Cleavers, the Bradys, and the Huxtables.

Another temptation to add too many values to your list comes when you hear what other families come up with. For instance, a family we know told us their core value was gratitude *(ooh, we should definitely add that one to ours!)* and another said theirs was humor *(how can we leave that off our list?),* and yet another claimed loyalty *(if we don't have that one, does it mean we don't care about one another?).*

While my wife and I certainly appreciate the blessings we've received, consider ourselves to have a sense of humor, and are committed to one another and to our family, we have to be honest and mature enough to recognize that gratitude, humor, and loyalty are not the strongest fundamental characteristics that make our family unique. We might say that we aspire to be even more appreciative, humorous, and loyal, but that is a far cry from the values that define and differentiate us.

STRATEGY

The other element of how a family can differentiate itself and identify its uniqueness is in the strategy that it chooses. What exactly does a strategy look like? It is nothing more than the two or three purposeful decisions a family makes that drives how it will live week by week, month by month, year by year.

The key to coming up with your strategic anchors is to acknowledge that it's a messy, inexact science, one that has no right answers. It requires an open mind and a willingness to engage in good discussion.

The best way to identify those anchors is to write down anything and everything that's true about your family, without classifying or categorizing it. Again, this is worth repeating: this is a messy process designed to help you get clarity, not an exercise in precision or exactitude. Your list will be made up of apples, oranges, bananas, and giraffes, and will probably have a number of items that are repetitive or duplicative. That's okay. Put it all down, and don't look back.

The family referred to earlier, which, again, served as a model for the Cousins family in the story, had a list that looked like the one below, and is presented in no particular order at all, because generating the list is meant to be a messy, organic process:

Four kids under age ten

Mom stays home

Dad has his own small services firm

No immediate family in the area

Active in their church

Kids attend Catholic school

Most of the parents' friends are parents of kids at the school

Dad runs for exercise

Mom goes to the gym

Mom is writing a musical as a hobby

Mom has an idea for working with preteen and teenage girls one day

They live in a ranch home in an older neighborhood

They go on vacation every summer with another family

Dad coaches the girls' basketball and soccer teams

Mom volunteers at school

Dad doesn't do work outside of the United States

Dad limits travel to five nights per month

Mom drives a minivan

Dad consults at church

Mom and dad talk to their parents often on the phone

Kids aren't allowed to have video games

Dad's office is ten minutes from home

Mom and dad pay a gardener to take care of yard

Mom and dad have cleaning ladies come twice per month

Mom has a babysitter come a few times a week to watch the younger kids so she can exercise, volunteer at school, and run errands

Older girls share a room

Family prays together every night

Family goes to church on Sundays

Family friends come over for dinner often

There are no TVs or computers in the kids' rooms

The house is often a little messy

The minivan is often more than a little messy

The garage is often really messy (never had a car in it)

They have two refrigerators

They have two sets of washers and dryers

Okay, that's a good start. Apples, oranges, pears, and giraffes. You include everything, large and small, regardless of whether it seems repetitive or incidental. Then you look at that list and you ask yourself if there are any overriding themes.

Eventually, and that means over the course of ten or fifteen minutes, the family in this example came up with the following themes.

Their lives are centered around their faith and church. They both volunteer there, their children attend school there, and many of their friends are parishioners and school parents there. And of course, their home prayer life fits into this as well, as does their commitment to try to treat others in a manner that is based on the teachings of Jesus Christ. Oh yeah, and the dad's firm does a lot of work with churches.

They try to maximize the time they spend with their children. That means mom works as a full-time mom and volunteers at school, dad limits his business travel and keeps it domestic to allow him to coach his daughters' sports teams. His office is within a few miles of home. Mom and dad don't feel guilty about outsourcing a few time-consuming chores (yard work, cleaning) so they can have the time they need to parent and coach and spend time with their children. They live below their means so that they aren't forced to have mom work outside the home to pay for extravagances that would require financial "stretching."

Because they don't live near their parents or siblings, they nurture family-like relationships with friends. They have people over for dinner often, go on vacation with other families, and provide help and rely on help from friends in every area of their lives. The godparents of their youngest daughter are family friends from school, and they are the godparents of another set of family friends from school. (Of course, they still love their parents and siblings; they just don't get to see them very often, which is why they call their parents a lot on the phone.)

And that is their strategy. Faith and church. Maximize time with kids. Substitute friends for day-to-day family members.

Is it the right strategy? Who knows? But it is the one they've *chosen* based on how they're living their lives and how they want to keep living. And it gives them clarity about how they will make decisions in the face of pressure to do and be what everyone else wants them to do and be.

And that's what we all need to do. What happens if you later come to the conclusion that you didn't identify the right themes or categories from your list? Change them. There is no deadline or final exam, and the only people who need to understand your strategy are the members of your family. A little change along the way is to be expected, if not encouraged.

So then, what is a family left with after clarifying its values and strategy? A paragraph. Two or three sentences that describe how that family is not exactly like any other family in the world.

We are a passionate family that believes in standing up strongly for what is right, even when there is a cost. We live our lives around our Church and our faith, placing special emphasis on maximizing our involvement in our children's lives, and nurturing family-like relationships with our friends.

That's it. Generally, directionally correct. Forget about grammar or sophistication or cleverness. It's not a slogan that requires wordsmithing. Just write down, in the plainest language possible, what makes your family who you are. The statement in the example is not going to win the Pulitzer Prize, and it didn't require a lot of editing. But it's certainly much clearer than what they had before, which was largely nothing.

Now, it's worth noting here that some families may have a value or a strategic anchor similar to yours, but none will have exactly the same paragraph, unless they're copying off of their neighbor's paper. Besides, what the family next door comes up with is not important. All that matters is that you've identified what it is about your family that makes you who you are.

More examples from real-life families can be found on page 204.

QUESTION #2

What is your family's top priority— rallying cry—right now?

nswering this question will provide the quickest and most dramatic sense of relief to frantic families. But it's key not to be distracted or intimidated by some new terminology—rallying cry, defining objectives, standard objectives—whatever you choose, the term should be as simple as it is liberating.

RALLYING CRY

Every family needs a single, agreed-upon top priority, something it can rally around for unity and maximum impact. The best way to determine that priority is to ask the right question in the manner that best provokes an honest, accurate answer. Here are some examples:

> "If we accomplish just one thing as a family before the Fourth of July, what would that be?"

"If there is one thing about our family that needs to be different by Christmas, what would it be?"

"What is it that we'd have to accomplish by the time that the school year starts in order for us to say that it was a successful summer?"

There are two keys to answering any of these questions. First, limit yourself to one primary answer. As difficult as that sounds, it is critical. How many times have you written a list of ten priorities only to look back later and realize that you've accomplished just three of them, and not the most difficult (a.k.a. important) ones at that?

The second key is to identify the right time frame, usually between two and six months. Why? Because anything longer than six months can seem so far into the future that it's tempting to procrastinate. *I might not even be working in this job in six months.* Or *maybe my daughter will grow out of this by then.* Anything shorter than two months is not enough time to make progress. *I want to rekindle my marriage by the end of the month. Oh, and refinance the house and clean out the garage, too.* Overly aggressive time frames, not to mention multiple top priorities, are recipes for disappointment and failure.

What might a typical answer look like?

There are no typical answers. Sometimes a rallying cry will be relatively tactical. *We need to finish our move into the new house by the end of September.* Or *we have to reorganize our finances and record keeping within the next three months.* Sometimes a rallying cry is broader and more foundational. *By the end of the year, we will have made a decision about whether to move to another state, or commit to staying here for the foreseeable future.* Or *in the next six months we will have turned around our poor health habits.*

Sometimes a rallying cry will revolve around one person in the family. Other times it will be limited to one particular activity or issue. The only thing that matters is that it is doable in the allotted time frame, and that the family understands that it is the single greatest priority for everyone.

Whenever I work with people who are trying to identify their rallying cry, I find that they are perplexed at first— for about three minutes. Suddenly, someone throws out an idea, and everyone starts thinking. Five minutes later, the answer seems overwhelmingly obvious.

Unfortunately, sometimes the answer that everyone agrees on first is either too broad or too tactical. In other words, the first attempt might really be a two-year goal, and so they need to come up with a more realistic, near-term rallying cry. Or maybe it's not broad or deep enough, and they need a longer-term goal.

A mom and dad in debt might say "we need to revamp our financial plan so that we can afford to send our kids to college and put money away for retirement." There is a decent chance that accomplishing that will take a number of years, and that a better, more realistic thematic goal might be "let's significantly reduce our day-to-day expenses."

Once that has been accomplished, then they might be able to think about the next steps.

Or perhaps that same mom and dad decide that their thematic goal should be "let's sell the car and buy one that costs less to run." Well, that may be one element of the plan, but it could easily be accomplished within a week. A better thematic goal, one that would warrant a longer time frame, would be, again, to reduce day-to-day expenses.

Now, it's important to realize that an outsider will not be able to read your rallying cry and tell if it is too broad and aggressive or too narrow and easy. Only you will know what is truly realistic and appropriate for your family. Luckily, it probably won't take you more than ten minutes to figure it out.

DEFINING OBJECTIVES

Don't be taken aback by the wonky nature of this section's title. Defining objectives are just the basic categories of things you'll have to do to achieve your rallying cry. Without identifying those categories, you'll be left with nothing but a general statement—and no context for getting it done.

So the family that decides to reduce living expenses might create the following defining objectives: trade in the gas hog, eat out less frequently, take a less extravagant vacation this year, refinance the house, postpone the kitchen remodel. Those are five specific and trackable activities that, if accomplished, will assure them of accomplishing their top priority.

STANDARD OBJECTIVES

This is another wonky title that need not alarm you. Standard objectives are just those regular, ongoing responsibilities that a family must pay attention to in order to keep its head above water. Without acknowledging these perennial responsibilities, families leave themselves open to getting surprised and distracted from their rallying cries.

For instance, as important as it might be for a family to cut back on daily living expenses, it can't do that in a way that jeopardizes fundamental needs of the family like health and education. And even if that family decides that its rallying cry should revolve around one particular child in the family, it must still attend to the basic, standard needs of the entire family.

Similarly, a company that decides to rally around changing its marketing message cannot simply ignore the need to continue selling its products, providing service to its customers, and retaining its employees. These are the standard objectives of the company, even if they aren't the top priority in that particular period.

Coming up with your family's standard objectives isn't usually difficult. That's because most families draw from a similar set of categories. These include financial health, physical health, spiritual health, marriage, education, social life, and fun. They might also include relationships with extended family, or maintenance of the home.

What's important about standard objectives is not that they differentiate your family but that they encompass those things that were important three years ago, last year, and this year, and will be important next year and three years from now. That way, when you identify and call out your rallying cry, you'll know you're being responsible by acknowledging your ongoing duties.

More examples from real-life families can be found on page 204.

QUESTION #3

How do you talk about and use the answers to these questions?

One of the most common mistakes people make when they do strategic planning or personal development plans is that they neatly produce a handsome document and bind it for posterity. It would be better to have your three-year-old write it in crayon on the kitchen wall, because at least then you would have to look at it from time to time. Fortunately, there is a better way to keep your uniqueness and top priority alive, one that doesn't involve crayons or defacing your kitchen. At least not much.

MEETINGS

The most important thing a family has to do to keep its context alive is discuss it in regular meetings. Yes, meetings.

As distasteful as that may sound, it is critical to talk about your context, and most important, regularly assess your progress against defining and standard objectives. How frequently? Every day is too often. Every month is not often enough. Weekly seems like a good idea because it gives you enough time to make progress during the week without removing a sense of urgency.

The key to making these meetings work is keeping them very, very short. Ten minutes should be enough, or maybe twenty if you're feeling like digging into your issues and getting something done. Anything longer and you'll find yourself skipping the meetings and forgetting about the whole process.

Start the meetings by going over the rallying cry, and then assess your progress against each of the defining objectives and standard objectives. Use a simple method for evaluating each area—I recommend assigning a color. Green means you're doing as well as possible, that you are either at or ahead of schedule. Yellow means you're doing okay but that there is some concern or risk if you don't keep pushing forward. Red means you're way behind and it needs immediate attention. And yes, if you have a hard time deciding between green and yellow, or yellow and red, then by all means, use lime green and orange.

Once you've rated your progress on each of the objectives (it should take three to five minutes), discuss those areas that are in need of attention. These will most likely be red or orange, or even yellow. Agree on what needs to be done that week to move those colors in a positive direction. And then, and this is key, end your meeting.

It will be tempting during your first meeting or two to keep talking and to go into great detail around some of the items on your list. I don't recommend this, because it will only create a memory of lengthy meetings that will make it that much harder for you to say, "Come on, let's do our Sunday night meeting." Even if you're climbing into bed and one of you realizes that you forgot to do the meeting, you can easily take ten additional minutes if you know that's really how long it will take.

Finally, there is the question of who should attend a family meeting. Of course, this depends on the nature of the family and the age of the children. An argument can be made that it should be the parents alone, because they are truly the leaders of the family. Then there is the argument that the whole family should come, so that they feel a part of planning and ownership for what the family is working toward. I think the answer, as it does so often, falls somewhere in between.

Kids don't need to be involved in identifying the values and strategy and goals. That truly is the parents' job as adults and leaders of the family. And clearly, some sensitive or complex family issues sometimes should not be addressed in front of children. All of this requires judgment, knowing when exposure gives kids greater perspective and confidence, and when it makes them feel vulnerable and afraid.

My recommendation would be to have the meetings with just the parents, and then talk to the kids about the meeting for a few minutes the next day. Show them what the family needs to focus on, and where progress is being made. But more important than any suggestion I can make is for me to encourage parents to use judgment and make decisions that will best enable the family to improve, not to adhere to some adage that may or may not apply.

VISIBILITY

Keeping your family plan visible is also critical. That means you need to find the best way to capture the information, and then find the right place in your home to display it.

Though I think it's important not to be overly prescriptive about how you capture and display your family context, I will make a suggestion here.

I recommend something that is neither overly permanent (carving it into your kitchen table isn't such a good idea) nor overly temporary (don't write it in dust on the refrigerator). Instead, get a whiteboard or a chalkboard or a bulletin board and write or type your context information on it, large enough to read from more than a few feet away.

Finally, I strongly suggest hanging your scoreboard near your family calendar so that you can have greater, more holistic context for the daily decisions you make about scheduling and activities. Ultimately, those decisions are what make our lives frantic.

Family Scoreboard

What is our top priority right now?

| Rallying Cry |

| Defining Objectives | Defining Objectives | Defining Objectives | Defining Objectives | Defining Objectives |

○   ○   ○   ○   ○

| Standard Objectives | Standard Objectives | Standard Objectives | Standard Objectives | Standard Objectives |

○   ○   ○   ○   ○

What makes us unique?

_____

_____

_____

How will we talk about and use the answers to this information?

_____

_____

_____

More examples from real-life families can be found on page 204.

AUTHOR'S NOTE

As I wrap this up, I feel the need to make a final confession, of sorts.

During much of the writing of this book I had moments of discomfort and guilt, prompted by two repeated internal questions: Are people who read this going to think that Laura and I have a neat house, perfectly behaved children, and a calm, purposeful, peaceful family? And if we don't, does that invalidate the lessons of the book?

The answers to those questions, of course, are *maybe* and *it depends.*

Some readers might mistakenly picture me sitting in my perfectly appointed office at home, writing peacefully about how other families can share our bliss if only they were as balanced and thoughtful as we are. Well, let me set the record straight.

First, our house is not particularly neat. In fact, the office where I've been writing lately has a slot car track snaking around the floor beneath my feet. This belongs to my boys, of course. We keep it in my office so that our toddler doesn't find it and tear it to shreds.

As for writing in peace, you need to know that my fourth graders are in the throes of their own writing project, a report on Alcatraz Island. They've been working about ten feet away from me, sprawled on my office floor so they can ask questions and share interesting bits of information about The Rock. (Did you know that the lighthouse on Alcatraz was the first one built on the West Coast?)

Which brings me to the second question that plagues me: Would it negate the lessons in this book if my family wasn't successful in using them? Well, to a certain extent, yes, it would. I mean, if we weren't able to extract real value from the methodology that I've laid out here, that wouldn't be a great endorsement of its value. Of course, this needs to be offset somewhat by the fact that it is always harder for authors or supposed experts to apply the principles of their work to their own families. I know that the last person who wants to have me lecture her on how to run her family is my wife. My parents would be close seconds.

Enough excuses. How are we doing? While I cannot deny that the Lencioni household continues to experience its fair share of stress—and we don't expect that to ever completely disappear—I am glad to report that by answering the questions laid out here, we have begun to productively channel that stress and obtain a real sense of progress and relief.

And while a certain amount of chaos remains, we're being much more purposeful now about which chaos to tolerate and which to squash. In fact, we've overcome some obstacles that we've been talking about and struggling with for years. My wife explained how the methodology in this book helped us do that.

"We're finally tackling these things now because they're part of our focused, stated priorities. When something is part of a bigger goal that I know we're going to be talking about every week, it's harder for me to let it get pushed aside by those pesky, tactical, and artificially urgent things that distract us from what really matters. Now I can let some things go that I would have felt guilty about ignoring in the past when everything was equally important. Now our family has real clarity."

And that, in a nutshell, is what this is all about.

FAMILY EXAMPLES

This section includes answers to the Three Big Questions from a variety of actual families I worked with in the development of this book. Their answers are provided to give readers a sense of the variety of ways that a family can use these ideas. Names have been changed to protect the innocent.

EXAMPLE 1: THE WATSON FAMILY

Brian and Sharon Watson have a thirteen-year-old boy and ten-year-old girl. Both parents work outside the home.

Question 1: What makes our family unique?

We value humor and incorporate it into every aspect of our lives. We believe in the importance of compassion and we treat others with respect and care. Finally, we are focused and passionate in our interests and pursuits.

Question 2: What is our family's most important priority—rallying cry—right now?

Between now and early spring, we will work on getting our teenaged son into private high school.

(Defining Objectives) To do that we will:

- Complete the application process and obtain recommendation letters.
- Support our son in maintaining schoolwork and good grades.
- Prepare our son emotionally for the transition into private school (departure from friends and so on).
- Adjust finances for school tuition.
- Prepare for logistics and transportation shift to school farther away (which will impact whole family).

(Standard Objectives) We will also have to stay on top of our regular responsibilities:

- Preserve marriage.
- Maintain quality family time, including extended family.
- Support kids in their activities.
- Take care of home administration.
- Exercise and maintain health.

Question 3: How will we use these answers and keep them alive?

We will discuss these issues as a couple during Friday night dinners, and then again as a family during our Sunday dinner family council meetings.

Author's Commentary

One of the most interesting aspects of the Watson family's rallying cry is its specificity: their thirteen-year-old son's admission to high school. Sometimes a rallying cry will be more general (for example, bring more balance to the family calendar), while for others it will be very specific (get Andrew into college). Both are fine approaches if they meet the needs of the family.

EXAMPLE 2: THE ROYAL FAMILY

Chris and Stacy Royal have two boys, ages nine and six. Stacy works full-time outside of the home and Chris stays home with the kids.

Question 1: What makes our family unique?

We are a family that values loyalty, respect, and hard work. The "family" unit is at the center of our lives. We spend much of our time together at home and at our family cabin. Dad stays at home until kids are school age and mom works full-time.

Question 2: What is our family's most important priority— rallying cry—right now?

In the next two months, we will work to create a more stable, supportive, and healthy environment for dad.

(Defining Objectives) To do that we will:

- Get control over (sick) grandfather's ongoing care.
- Work on youngest son's discipline.
- Establish a consistent exercise and workout schedule.
- Consider counseling or therapy.
- Begin thinking about next steps in his career.
- Mom and dad will spend more quality time together— thinking and talking.

(Standard Objectives) We will also have to stay on top of our regular responsibilities:

- Finances
- Family health
- Fun
- Marriage
- Education

Question 3: How will we use these answers and keep them alive?

During our "date night" we will dedicate the first fifteen minutes to discussing our rallying cry.

Author's Commentary

There are a few things that are interesting about the Royal family's answers. Like the Watsons', their rallying cry is also specific, but this time centered around the general health of one of the parents. I've found this to be fairly common in families, where the mom or dad is in need of attention. Additionally, there are six different elements of their defining objectives, which is more than most families have, but entirely appropriate.

EXAMPLE 3: THE HILTON FAMILY

Rick and Andrea Hilton have a six-year-old boy and a three-year-old girl. Both parents work outside the home.

Question 1: What makes our family unique?

We are a family that puts heart into everything we do. We value gratitude and believe that we should treat others as we would like to be treated. We are a family that spends a lot of time together, opens our home to friends and extended family, and has spirited discussions about life.

Question 2: What is our family's most important priority—rallying cry—right now?

Between now and the end of summer, we will consolidate and simplify our lives.

(Defining Objectives) To do that we will:
- Sell rental house.
- Finish financial planning.
- Reduce dad's non-work commitments.
- Keep mom sane during midlife crisis.
- Clean garage and purge house.

(Standard Objectives) We will also have to stay on top of our regular responsibilities:
- Quality family time
- Marriage
- Home administration (bills paid, homework done)
- Personal and spiritual growth

Question 3: How will we use these answers and keep them alive?

We will talk every morning over coffee and review the above once a week, on Sunday afternoon.

Author's Commentary

This is a classic rallying cry, one that is fairly comprehensive but provides specifics about how to accomplish the overall goal.

EXAMPLE 4: THE SHANNON FAMILY

Tom and Mary Shannon have two boys, ages ten and seven. Tom works full-time, and Mary is a stay-at-home mom.

Question 1: What makes our family unique?

We try to emphasize that it takes hard work and focused effort to succeed. But winning outright is not the only measure. As long as someone contributes their best effort (in all ways) then they are tracking to become the best version of themselves and should feel proud. Winning is great but not required. Likewise, just showing up is no cause for celebration or reward.

Question 2: What is our family's most important priority—rallying cry—right now?

Between now and the end of school, our primary goal is to help encourage our two young boys to have and demonstrate more self-control. To us, this means stopping what they are doing when asked (video games, playing, reading, and so on) and doing what an adult asks them to do right away and without whining, negotiating, or stalling.

(Defining Objectives) To do that we will:

- Give praise when they do the right thing on their own.
- Create a system where they earn their "electronics time" on the weekend—after showing self-control when needed during the school week.
- Emphasize via dinner-time conversations how mom and dad show self-control regarding their activities.
- Opportunistically discuss movie characters, sports heroes, and other role models as more examples of how it takes hard work and focused effort to succeed.

**(Standard Objectives) We will also have to stay
on top of our regular responsibilities:**

- Faith
- Health
- Marriage
- Finances
- Education

Question 3: How will we use these answers and keep them alive?
Every Sunday afternoon we will have a ten-minute meeting to
assess how well we're doing.

Author's Commentary
What is interesting about the Shannon family's rallying cry is that
it is something that every family, and every parent, wants to do.
But to give themselves the best chance of success, they're making it their top priority for a given period of time. Too often, families keep talking about and working on discipline of their kids,
but they mix it in with every other top priority and never really
see meaningful results. Also, the Shannons have a longer and
more detailed description of their rallying cry, which is fine.
Whatever helps them understand what they're trying to accomplish is appropriate.

EXAMPLE 5: THE EUGENE FAMILY

Victor and Nancy Eugene have a twelve-year-old girl and an eight-year-old boy. Victor works full-time, and Nancy works part-time.

Question 1: What makes our family unique?

We live a bi-cultural life, splitting time between Puerto Rico and the United States. We travel regularly and expose our kids to as many different cultures and concepts as possible. We maintain close relationships with friends and family around the world and try to visit as often as possible.

Question 2: What is our family's most important priority— rallying cry—right now?

Within the next two months, we will improve the overall strength and health of our family.

(Defining Objectives) To do that we will:

- Identify the cause of our son's learning struggle.
- Reduce the number of activities our son is involved in.
- Mom and dad will start doing weekly date nights to talk.
- Mom and dad will exercise and eat healthier and get physical exams.
- Postpone mom's plans for a career change.

(Standard Objectives) We will also have to stay on top of our regular responsibilities:

- Education
- Health
- Extended family and friends
- Faith
- Marriage
- Finances

Question 3: How will we use these answers and keep them alive?

We'll review our defining objectives during weekly dates.

Author's Commentary

Here is another unique and entirely appropriate example. Notice that the last defining objective has to do with postponing an activity in order to better focus on a different one. One of the powerful parts of having a rallying cry and defining objectives is giving yourself permission to stop doing something until the most important priority is achieved.

EXAMPLE 6: THE SORENSEN FAMILY

Don and Mary Jane Sorensen are empty nesters with three children and six grandchildren. Both Sorensens work.

Question 1: What makes our family unique?

We are a hardworking family committed to traditional values. Our marriage, our kids, and now our grandkids are at the core of our existence.

Question 2: What is our family's most important priority— rallying cry—right now?

Between now and the end of the year, we will begin to prepare for retirement.

(Defining Objectives) To do that we will:

- Sell investment property.
- Work with financial planner to establish a retirement budget.
- Determine a schedule to ensure we stay active.
- Establish an exit strategy for work.
- Deal with the emotional aspects of retirement.

(Standard Objectives) We will also have to stay on top of our regular responsibilities:

- Marriage
- Extended family
- Finances
- Health
- Faith

Question 3: How will we use these answers and keep them alive?
We will review our family clarity during weekend drives to our second home.

Author's Commentary
This example is unique because it deals with empty-nesters on the verge of retirement. And yet, it applies in much the same way.

EXAMPLE 7: ANDREA

Andrea is a single woman in her twenties.

Question 1: What makes me unique?

I am a person striving to build a life built on my faith in God. I strongly value my small network of close friends. My need for a creative outlet is core to who I am as a person. It is very important to me to maintain close relationships with my remote family.

Question 2: What is my most important priority— rallying cry—right now?

I need to establish a sense of permanence in my residence in California.

(Defining Objectives) To do that I will:

- Strengthen my local community of faith and friends.
- Establish a regular schedule of family visits and communication.
- Establish a realistic financial budget.
- Develop a regular schedule of activities to maintain balance.

(Standard Objectives) I will also have to stay on top of my regular responsibilities:

- Work at a healthy lifestyle.
- Maintain consistent communication and quality time with close friends.
- Maintain regular communication with family members.
- Continue to deepen my faith life.

Question 3: How will I use these answers and keep them alive?

I will clearly post my objectives for easy reminding. Additionally, I will reevaluate my progress weekly and revisit my rallying cry in June.

Author's Commentary

Here is an example of a single person using the model to focus her time and energy around what matters most to her. Even a person without kids running around the house can feel unfocused and frantic, and can benefit from clarity about what is most important for them in a given time period.

ACKNOWLEDGMENTS

The first person I want to acknowledge and thank is my dad, who passed from this earth just before this book was finished. You were a rock throughout my life, Dad, and an unselfish source of time and energy and support. I miss you.

And I want to thank my mom who, along with my dad, showed me what it means to be a dedicated parent and to put family before everything else. How you managed our homework, sports, activities, and household I'll never know.

Of course I want to acknowledge my wife, Laura, for your complete dedication to our boys, and your unwavering support for me and my work. Sharing the responsibility for managing our frantic family has been my sleepless privilege, one that I will always treasure.

I want to thank my wonderful friends and coworkers at The Table Group—Amy, Tracy, Michele, Karen, Jeff, Lynne, Alison, Danielle, and Jackie. You are like family to me, and your advice and counsel and patience and inspiration and energy are more important to me than you will ever realize.

I also appreciate your willingness to share stories about your families, which has been a source of great inspiration and humor to me.

I thank my dear brother and sister for your passion and commitment to our family, especially this year. And to my many aunts, uncles, cousins, and relatives for your love and concern this year too.

I thank my editor, Susan, and all her colleagues at Jossey-Bass/Wiley, both in San Francisco and New York, for your commitment to my books and to all of us at The Table Group. And I thank Rita for her special help with public relations, and Jim for being so much more than just an agent.

And a special thanks to Tracy for your commitment to this book, and for your great attention to detail.

I want to acknowledge and express my appreciation to the many families that served as guinea pigs of sorts for this book: the Amadors, the De Witts, the Fiorindos, the Gibsons, the Hietts, the Hourigans, the Magues, the Neveses, the Nobles, the Phillipses, and the Rangos.

And most important, as always, I reserve my deepest gratitude to God, the Father, Son, and Holy Spirit, for providing all that is good, and for the many blessings bestowed on my family.

ABOUT THE AUTHOR

Patrick Lencioni is a *New York Times* best-selling business author of seven books including *The Five Dysfunctions of a Team* and *The Three Signs of a Miserable Job*. He is also president and founder of The Table Group, a firm that develops new ideas for making organizations more effective. In addition to his writing, Pat is one of America's leading keynote speakers and a sought-after consultant to CEOs and teams at various organizations including large, multinational companies, start-ups, and non-profits. Clients who have engaged his services include Southwest Airlines, General Mills, Chick-fil-A, Newell Rubbermaid, Cox Communications, Microsoft, and the U.S. Military Academy, West Point, to name a few.

At home, in the San Francisco Bay Area, Pat and his wife Laura are busy raising four boys under the age of eleven. They volunteer at St. Isidore School and Church, coach Mustang Soccer, CYO Basketball, and San Ramon Valley Little League Baseball.

To learn more about Patrick and The Table Group, please visit www.tablegroup.com.

The Three Big Questions for a Frantic Family

For Frantic Family tools, downloads, and products visit

www.thefranticfamily.com

The Table Group is dedicated to helping organizations of all kinds function more effectively through better leadership, teamwork, and overall health.

the table group
a patrick lencioni company

www.tablegroup.com 925.299.9700